Coxheath Library
Heath Road
xheath
Maidstone) 74

COX

D0834012

C333626332

LISTELLANY

LISTELLANY

A miscellany
of very British top tens,
from politics to pop

John Rentoul

First published 2014 by
Elliott and Thompson Limited
27 John Street, London WC1N 2BX
www.eandtbooks.com

ISBN: 978-1-78396-004-0

Copyright © John Rentoul 2014

All rights reserved. No part of this publication may be reproduced, stored
in or introduced into a retrieval system, or transmitted, in any form,
or by any means (electronic, mechanical, photocopying, recording or
otherwise) without the prior written permission of the publisher. Any
person who does any unauthorized act in relation to this publication may
be liable to criminal prosecution and civil claims for damages.

Extract on pages 81–82 reproduced, with permission, from *Blackadder
Goes Forth*, created by Richard Curtis, Rowan Atkinson, John Lloyd and
Ben Elton. Script written by Richard Curtis and Ben Elton.

9 8 7 6 5 4 3 2 1

A catalogue record for this book is available from the British Library.

Typesetting: Marie Doherty
Printed in the UK by TJ International Ltd.

CONTENTS

TOP TEN REASONS TO READ THIS BOOK (OR 'THE INTRODUCTION')

1. Lists are the future of journalism, the internet and therefore the world.

2. Lists are also the past. Ten-item lists in particular have a history that goes back to even before the word 'listicle' was coined. Moses's top ten dos and don'ts was a handy way of summarising the rules for an entire society.

3. The lists in this book are totally fascinating. Did you know that 'male' and 'female' are not related to each other (deriving from Latin *masculus* and *femella*), while 'man' and 'woman' (man and wife-man in Old English) are? If you are not completely entranced by this, you will like something else here. Genuine shop names including Melon Cauli and Napoleon Boiler Parts? Go on.

4. The lists in this book will make you cleverer. Worried about the distractability of the internet? Looking up from the screen after 17 minutes wondering, yet again, what it was you meant to look up in the first place? Here is highly educational material presented in concentrated form, and anyone can pay attention for just ten points.

5. But let us not be purely utilitarian. One of the purposes of education is the joy of learning for its own sake. Herein is distilled the joy of language, music and politics.

6. Also quite a bit of pedantry (tautologies, misquotations), Britishness (the most English remarks of all time, best British

place names), literature (best first and last lines) and films (turkeys that are actually quite good).

7. Curiosity is good for you. My friend Ian Leslie has written a whole book about it (*Curious: The Desire to Know and Why Your Future Depends on It*). I have compiled a whole book of things for you to be curious about.

8. You may have missed one or two of these lists when they first appeared in the *New Review*, the *Independent on Sunday* magazine, since May 2013, or you may, having had your appetite whetted, want to see all the things that didn't make the top ten in each category but that are nevertheless brilliant. A bit like how, in the old days, I disdained music that was 'too popular' and preferred my favourite singles to peak in the lower reaches of the Top Forty.

9. There are top tens here that have never before appeared in print: world exclusives listing upbeat songs that tell a sad story, translated tautologies (Sahara means desert, and what not), words that lost or gained an 'n' (such as a norange or an ewt), surnames that have died out and everyday lies (such as 'It won't take a minute').

10. You want to know about stupid car names, don't you? There really is a car called the Mazda Bongo Friendee.

For more top tens and debates, visit www.listellany.com

UNDERRATED FAMILY FILMS

When I watched *The Emperor's New Groove* again after several years I could not believe what a great film it is. Fine plot, great characters, quick and clever dialogue, uses pre-computer-generated imagery (CGI) brilliantly – and yet it is almost forgotten.

1. *The Emperor's New Groove*, Disney, 2000. Incan emperor is turned into a llama and taught a lesson: majestic.

2. *Basil The Great Mouse Detective*, Disney, 1986. 'Big Ben fight scene, robot mouse Queen Victoria and a peg-legged bat. What's not to like?' It was the first film Mark Wallace saw.

3. *Megamind*, DreamWorks, 2010. Unoriginal? I thought it was great, and morally subtle.

4. *Monster in Paris*, English version released 2012. Surprisingly affecting dub of the French original.

5. *Jumanji*, 1995. Supernatural board game in which wild animals come to life? Sounds dire, but it was Tom Doran's childhood favourite.

6. *Small Soldiers*, DreamWorks, 1998. '*Toy Story* with heavier firepower,' says Gaz W.

7. *Robin Hood*, Disney, 1973. Unfairly overlooked, overshadowed by predecessors *The Jungle Book* and *Aristocats*.

8. *Atlantis: The Lost Empire*, Disney, 2001. Another cartoon classic overshadowed by computer-generated imagery blockbusters to come.

9. *Flushed Away*, Aardman/DreamWorks, 2006. Terrible title; outstanding plot, characters and CGI.

10. *Lion King II: Simba's Pride*, Disney, 1998. Surprisingly high-quality, straight-to-video sequel.

PLURALS THAT HAVE BECOME SINGULAR

It is a little old-fashioned to use data, dice, graffiti, panini, media and politics as plural nouns these days, and I know only one person who treats news as a plural, but we are dimly aware that these words were not always as singular as they are now. However, Rich Greenhill, a virtuoso of language curios, came up with many other words that were once – unknown to me – plurals. Here are the best…

1. **Quince** Middle English plural of Old French *cooin*, from Latin for apple of Cydonia, now Chania, Crete.

2. **Stamina** Latin plural of *stamen*, thread or essential element, before it was applied by analogy to flower parts.

3. **Chintz** Plural of chint, a stained or painted calico cloth imported from India, from Hindi *chimt*, spattering, stain.

4. **Pox** Plural of pock, as in pock-marked.

5. **Truce** Plural of true, Middle English, in the sense of belief, trust.

6. **Invoice** Plural of obsolete invoy, from French *envoy, envoyer*, to send.

7. **Broccoli** Italian, plural of *broccolo*, cabbage sprout, head, diminutive of *brocco*, shoot.

8. **Dismal** Originally a noun, for the two days in each month which were believed to be unlucky, from Anglo-Norman French *dis mal*, and medieval Latin *dies mali*, evil days.

9. **Sweden** Originally a plural of Swede, a Swedish person.

10. **Bodice** Originally bodies.

Greenhill also pointed out that MMR – measles, mumps and rubella – are all plurals:

11. Measles. Middle English maseles, probably from Middle Dutch *masel*, pustule. The spelling change was due to association with Middle English mesel, leprous, leprosy.

12. Mumps. Late 16th century: from obsolete mump, meaning grimace, have a miserable expression.

13. Rubella. Modern Latin neuter plural of *rubellus*, reddish.

Just to show off, he said – again, I had no idea – that the words primate and termite arose from mistaking the three-syllable Latin plurals *primates* and *termites* (the singulars being *primas* and *termes*) for two-syllable words. The *Oxford Dictionary* doesn't specifically support this, but it seems plausible.

14. Chess. Middle English: from Old French *esches*, plural of *eschec*, check, which in the sense of holding back or verifying comes from the game of chess. I did not know that.

15. Delicatessen

16. Lasagne

17. Agenda. Latin: 'things to be done'.

18. Candelabra

19. WAG: stands for wives and girlfriends (mostly of famous footballers) but is often used as a singular, 'a WAG'.

FOOTNOTES

This list arose after I praised the wonder of the footnotes in John Campbell's biography of Roy Jenkins, a fabulous old-fashioned book, with starred footnotes at the bottom of the page, plus numbered endnotes, including endnotes in footnotes.

1. 'It [is] wearisome to add "except the Italians" to every generalisation. Henceforth it may be assumed.' A. J. P. Taylor, *The Struggle for Mastery in Europe, 1848–1918*.

2. **'Strengthened, I should have thought spoiled, by whisky.'** Roy Jenkins, in *Gladstone*, on Queen Victoria's preference for claret.

3. **'Trees didn't burst into flame ... A better simile would be "not like molten gold".'** A footnote to: 'Sunlight poured like molten gold across the ... landscape.' Terry Pratchett, *The Light Fantastic*.

4. **'...his trousers were creased at the sides not front and back.'** A. J. P. Taylor on King George V, in *English History 1914–45*.

5. **'Despite Orwell's expressed wishes, the ... Uniform Edition includes three semi-colons.'** A footnote to: '*Coming Up for Air* hasn't got a semi-colon in it.' Peter Davison, editor, *George Orwell: A Life in Letters*.

6. **'"You're fired" were the exact words as I remember them.'** A footnote to: 'My first job ended when the editor said something to me that made it impossible to go on working for him.' Christopher Hitchens, *Hitch-22*.

7. **'This is the only reference in the canon to Holmes's eyebrows.'** Leslie S. Klinger, editor, *The New Annotated Sherlock Holmes*.

8. **'It is one of the mysteries of existence that what is called red tape is in fact pink.'** Profs George Gretton and Kenneth Reid, on a quirk of title deeds, in *Conveyancing (2nd Edition)*.

9. **'Haemophilia is, like the enlargement of the prostate, an exclusively male disorder. But not in this work.'** Samuel Beckett, *Watt*.

10. 'They discovered a problem ... with the [website]: investorsexchange.com' A footnote to: 'The Investors Exchange, which wound up being shortened to IEX.' Michael Lewis, *Flash Boys*.

MALAPROPISMS

This one was Nick Thornsby's idea. As Mrs Malaprop says in Sheridan's play *The Rivals*, 'If I reprehend anything in this world it is the use of my oracular tongue, and a nice derangement of epitaphs.'

1. 'She's as headstrong as an allegory on the banks of the Nile.' Mrs Malaprop.

2. 'It's great to be back on terra cotta.' John Prescott after a stormy flight, 1999.

3. 'I am a person who recognises the fallacy of humans.' George W. Bush to Oprah Winfrey.

4. 'The world is your lobster, my son.' Arthur Daley, *Minder*.

5. 'I'm as happy as a sandbag.' A friend of Alistair Gray's. 'She has an unconscious gift. She also said something was "a bit of a damp squid"'.

6. 'Cow-towing to the Americans.' *Daily Telegraph* report of criticism of New Labour by Ian Davidson, Labour MP. Did this involve pulling cattle behind a boat?

7. 'He eludes confidence.' William Bratton, Los Angeles police chief, of Barack Obama's second inaugural speech, 2009.

8. 'It's not rocket fuel.' Henry McLeish, former Scottish First Minister, to John Swinney, SNP leader.

9. 'If I don't want to serve someone, that is my provocative.' Landlord to Lloyd Bracey, who worked in a pub as a student.

10. 'Chocolate peripherals' Hugh Kellett's great aunt's dessert order.

Also nominated:

11. Deferring payments would 'only be playing smokes and daggers'. Bertie Ahern, former Irish prime minister. A top ten of malapropisms by Ahern alone could have been compiled, including 'hindsight is 50/50 vision' and the not-yet-authenticated 'upsetting the apple tart'.

12. 'When I find the allegator concerned.' American general rejecting damaging anonymous claims. Allegedly.

13. 'I've got a head like a sore bear.'

14. 'It's not the sanity of picket lines that bothers me, it's the sanity of human life.' John Prescott, 2002.

15. 'I'll see you at the Duke of Windsor at 6 o'clock, then.' 'Right, we'll sympathise watches.' Two men exiting a pub after what may well have been a long drinking session, overheard by Roger Stevenson.

16. 'Councillor, come up here and rest your papers on the rectum.' Chairman of Stevenage district council, according to former councillor Peter Metcalfe.

17. 'He's as honest as the day is blue.'

SIGNS WITH DOUBLE MEANINGS

Mike Graham said, 'I refuse to go in here,' when he posted a picture of a door in New York with the sign, 'Refuse Room'. As Tom Freeman pointed out, 'That was the policy of the Bethlehem innkeeper.' Here are ten more signs with unintended messages.

1. **This door is alarmed** But the sign doesn't say what is bothering it.

2. **Disabled toilet** Whenever Andrew Denny sees it, he thinks, 'Well, why doesn't someone fix it, then?'

3. **'Women'** Sign on ladies' loo, with alarming quotation marks.

4. **Dogs must be carried** On London Underground escalators: an obscure grammatical trap, suggesting that no one without a dog in their arms or in a bag is permitted.

5. **We don't fly in our chickens. They're 100% British** In unidentified supermarket.

6. **Eggs buzz at gate** Seen outside a farmhouse in Hadlow Down, East Sussex.

7. **Slow Children Playing** Faster children, of course, can get out of the way in time.

8. **Children: Please Drive Slowly** Boy and girl racers alert.

9. **Train drivers must not be disturbed** At London Bridge station.

10. **If this lift is found to be out of order please use an alternative lift** Manchester Piccadilly station. The second meaning being, 'Get lost.'

There were many good entries, so here are the next ten:

11. Humped zebra crossing. Worth waiting for this camel hybrid.

12. To avoid suffocation keep away from children. They use up all the oxygen.

13. Self Storage. 'Who wants to do this?' asked Jenifer Jeffery.

14. Heavy plant crossing. Look out for triffids.

15. Quiet birds have ears. Sign outside a hide at the London Wetland Centre bird reserve.

16. No Parking Cars Will Be Clamped. On the walls of the car park next to Bristol Museum.

17. Agent has no money. 'At each kiosk service window in our regional subway, Bay Area Rapid Transit.' Fred Walker, who thought this may be an invitation to charity.

18. Fire Fighting Lift. 'Sign above a lift in my office. The idea of the lift fighting the fire has tickled me ever since I noticed it,' says Peter Shearman.

19. Baggage trolleys must not be taken onto the platform for safety reasons. Heathrow Terminal 4 (Piccadilly Line), and at Gatwick Airport (National Rail). Taking them onto the platform for other reasons is, of course, fine.

20. Post No Bills. 'I always thought the sign was a request to postmen meaning the rest of the post could be delivered, but not the bills.' Simon Cox.

SURPRISINGLY UNRELATED PAIRS OF WORDS

My favourite list in the whole book. I did not believe that there were as many as ten examples of surprisingly unrelated words, thinking 'female/male' and 'island/isle' quite enough excitement for one language. Many thanks to Rich Greenhill, whose numbers four to seven proved me wrong.

1. **Female, not related to male** Female is from the Latin *femella*, a diminutive of *femina*, a woman; while male is from the Old French *masle*, from the Latin *masculus*.

2. **Island, isle** Old English iegland, ieg, from a base meaning

watery, according to the *Oxford Dictionary*. The 's' came by association with isle, from the Latin *insula* via Old French.

3. **Outrage, rage** From Old French *ou(l)trage*, based on Latin *ultra*, beyond.

4. **Uproar, roar** Middle Dutch *oproer*, from *op*, meaning up, and *roer*, meaning confusion.

5. **Bridegroom, groom** Old English brydguma, from bryd, bride, and guma, man. The change in the second syllable influenced by groom.

6. **Pickaxe, axe** Middle English pikoys, from Old French *picois*, related to pike. The change in the ending was influenced by axe.

7. **Gingerbread, bread** Gingerbread originally meant preserved ginger used to make the biscuit, from Old French *gingembrat*, from medieval Latin *gingibratum*, from *gingiber,* ginger.

8. **Belfry, bell** Belfry was originally a watchtower, from French *berfrei*, but because it had bells, it acquired an 'l'.

9. **Muskrat, musk** The animal does produce a musky smell, but the word is actually from Algonquin for 'red'.

10. **Crayfish, fish** From Old French *crevice*, related to German *Krebs*, crab. The ending altered by association with fish in about the 16th century.

And one more:

11. 'Jubilee' and 'jubilation' come from different sources. The first comes via Latin from the Hebrew *yōome*, which

means trumpet blast, with which the year of emancipation and restoration in Judaism is proclaimed every fifty years. The second comes from Latin *jubilat-*, 'called out', used by Christian writers to mean 'shouted for joy', from *jubilare*.

FIRST SENTENCES OF NOVELS

Jonny Geller, the boss of the literary agency Curtis Brown, said, 'This is the saddest story I have ever heard,' from *The Good Soldier* by Ford Madox Ford, is 'perhaps my favourite opening sentence in fiction.' Here are ten more I like.

1. 'There was a boy called Eustace Clarence Scrubb, and he almost deserved it.' C. S. Lewis, *The Voyage of the Dawn Treader*.

2. 'Marley was dead: to begin with.' Charles Dickens, *A Christmas Carol*. Also contains the finest use of a colon in literature.

3. 'The scent, smoke and sweat of a casino are nauseating at three in the morning.' Ian Fleming, *Casino Royale*.

4. 'There were four of us.' Jerome K. Jerome, *Three Men in a Boat*.

5. 'It was a queer, sultry summer, the summer they electro-cuted the Rosenbergs, and I didn't know what I was doing in New York.' Sylvia Plath, *The Bell Jar*. I do like the inversion

of the first part of the sentence, which makes it seem as if the strange weather were more important than the Rosenbergs' execution, followed by the deadpan twist of the second part.

6. '**All this happened, more or less.**' Kurt Vonnegut, *Slaughterhouse Five*.

7. '**It was a bright cold day in April, and the clocks were striking thirteen.**' George Orwell, *Nineteen Eighty-Four*.

8. '**It was the day my grandmother exploded.**' Iain Banks, *The Crow Road*.

9. '**Cities at night, I feel, contain men who cry in their sleep and then say Nothing.**' Martin Amis, *The Information*.

10. '**It was a dark, blustery afternoon in spring, and the city of London was chasing a small mining town across the dried-out bed of the old North Sea.**' Philip Reeve, *Mortal Engines*. A cliché in the opening phrase brilliantly subverted by the shock of a city pursuing a small town.

This was a popular list – although the 140-character limit winnowed entries somewhat. Even so, I received many representations on behalf of books that people thought should have been in the list.

Lots of people thought Anthony Burgess ought to have been in it. You know, the silly one about the archbishop and the catamite. No.

There were also many nominations for the sonorous but meaningless first sentence of *A Tale of Two Cities*. Worst of sentences, certainly.

Janan Ganesh tried to sneak this past me: 'The world is what it is; men who are nothing, who allow themselves to become nothing, have no place in it.' V. S. Naipaul, *A Bend in the River*. Definitely not. Even if it meant anything, it has a semi-colon in it. Inexcusable.

Others had more promising suggestions. Owen Bennett liked this, saying it 'sets up inverted emotions': 'People are afraid to merge on freeways in Los Angeles.' Bret Easton Ellis, *Less Than Zero*. Yes, it has something. Not sure about the inverted emotions, but it is a good first sentence that makes you think and want to read the next.

Daniel Hannan said he was 'shocked – shocked – not to see': 'In a hole in the ground there lived a hobbit.' I know what he means. I share his admiration for Tolkien, although in my case it is mixed with two things. One is the reaction identified by Terry Pratchett: 'Put in one lousy dragon and they call you a fantasy writer.' The other is that it is, when it comes to it, a children's book.

Adrian Hilton said he was disappointed not to see: 'The past is a foreign country: they do things differently there.' L. P. Hartley, *The Go-Between*. That is a good one. It even contains a fine colon, although not as special as that in the first sentence of *A Christmas Carol*. I may have reacted against it because it has become almost as clichéd as blokes with fortunes being in want of wives or the heterogeneity of unhappy families.

Matthew Hoffman's favourite first sentence is: 'The sun shone, having no alternative, on the nothing new.' Samuel Beckett, *Murphy*. On rediscovering it, I was surprised to come across the second 'the', which diminishes it slightly. But yes, it is a contender.

Clive Davis and David Paxton offered first drafts of first sentences. Davis noted that the opening of *Nineteen Eighty-Four* was originally: 'It was a cold, blowy day in early April and a million radios were striking thirteen.' While Paxton pointed out that Ian Fleming's first attempt at the start of *Casino Royale* was: 'Scent and smoke and sweat hit the taste buds with an acid thwack at three o'clock in the morning.' Both examples illustrate the virtue of rewriting.

Finally, John McTernan pointed out that I had failed to include this: 'If I am out of my mind, it's all right with me, thought Moses Herzog.' Saul Bellow, *Herzog*. Best ever. Don't know how I missed that one.

LAST SENTENCES OF NOVELS

Guy Keleny, my colleague, had no suggestions for opening lines, but said that he rather liked the last sentence of *The Lord of the Rings*. Single, complete sentences with a 140-character limit turned out to be quite restrictive, but, with the usual warning about spoilers, here we go …

1. 'Well, I'm back.' *The Lord of the Rings* by J. R. R. Tolkien.

2. **'It could be that the sort of sentence one wants right here is the kind that runs, and laughs, and slides, and stops right on a dime.'** *Speedboat* by Renata Adler. A lovely line that even

discusses what sort of sentence it is and that imitates itself, gently mocking.

3. 'After all, tomorrow is another day.' *Gone with the Wind* by Margaret Mitchell.

4. 'Ever drifting down the stream—/ Lingering in the golden gleam—/ Life, what is it but a dream?' *Through the Looking-Glass* by Lewis Carroll.

5. 'He passed on unsuspected and deadly, like a pest in the street full of men.' *The Secret Agent* by Joseph Conrad.

6. 'So we beat on, boats against the current, borne back ceaselessly into the past.' *The Great Gatsby* by F. Scott Fitzgerald.

7. 'Just watch me.' *The Woman Upstairs* by Claire Messud.

8. 'There was a point to this story, but it has temporarily escaped the chronicler's mind.' *So Long and Thanks for All the Fish* by Douglas Adams.

9. 'She was seventy-five and she was going to make some changes in her life.' *The Corrections* by Jonathan Franzen.

10. 'You could see a long way – but not as far as Velma had gone.' *Farewell, My Lovely* by Raymond Chandler.

My insistence on single, complete sentences ruled out some promising entries:

'Don't ever tell anybody anything. If you do, you start missing everybody.' J. D. Salinger, *The Catcher in the Rye*.

'Now vee may perhaps to begin. Yes?' Philip Roth, *Portnoy's Complaint*. The whole book is Portnoy's monologue to his psychiatrist. This is the only thing the psychiatrist says.

The 140-character limit also cut off some popular nominations including George Orwell's *Animal Farm* and Aldous Huxley's *Brave New World*. It also ruled out of order that James Joyce one that ends yes I said yes I will Yes, which is not bad as a last line, although as a last sentence goes on a bit.

Of those that made the final cut, *The Great Gatsby* was subject to late appeals, including from my friend Matt Hoffman, a former colleague at the *Independent* and literary editor of *Time Out* in the 1970s: 'Isn't this metaphor, literally, backwards? The past is the source of the river, the future is where it's going.' These objections were overruled. I always thought it referred to a tidal estuary. The direction doesn't matter: the point is the struggle to prevent the current carrying you where you don't want to go. Anyway, it's poetic licence, isn't it?

So to those that didn't make it:

'Happiness is but an occasional episode in a general drama of pain.' Thomas Hardy, *Mayor of Casterbridge*. A good encapsulation of Hardy's cheerful approach to life rather than a great last sentence of its own.

'Yet what is any ocean but a multitude of drops?' David Mitchell, *Cloud Atlas*. Ho hum.

'The song died away; they heard the river, bearing down

the snows of winter into the Mediterranean.' E. M. Forster, *A Room with a View*. Pleasant but inconsequential.

'We shall sit with lighter bosoms on the hearth, to see the ashes of our fires turn gray and cold.' Charles Dickens, *Hard Times*. Don't like it.

'The knife came down, missing him by inches, and he took off.' Joseph Heller, *Catch-22*. Nominated by John Blake. One of my favourite books, but the sentence itself means little without all that goes before.

'It was the devious cruising Rachel, that in her retracing search after her missing children, only found another orphan.' Herman Melville, *Moby-Dick*. Not my kind of thing.

'Somebody threw a dead dog after him down the ravine.' Malcolm Lowry, *Under the Volcano*. All right in an absurdist way.

'After a while I went out and left the hospital and walked back to the hotel in the rain.' Ernest Hemingway, *A Farewell to Arms*. Brian Millar said this is a fabulous piece of underwriting, and that Hemingway wrote forty-seven variations. Well, it is certainly underwritten.

'And that's that.' J. B. Priestley, *Angel Pavement*. Good, but too short and obvious.

'It is a far, far better thing that I do, than I have ever done; it is a far, far better rest that I go to than I have ever known.' Charles Dickens, *A Tale of Two Cities*. Lots of nominations. Not in a million years.

WORDS THAT USED TO MEAN THE OPPOSITE

Balustrade and banister both come from the same root: *balaustion*, Greek for wild pomegranate flower, because of pillars that resemble its curving calyx tube. Which has nothing to do with anything, but is a curiosity that I like. Sometimes, though, words come so far from their origins that they end up meaning the opposite of when they started.

1. **Respect** As in, 'With respect'.

2. **Humbled** The late Simon Hoggart noted its modern use in thank-you speeches.

3. **Nice** Meant 'stupid' in Middle English (from *nescius*, Latin for ignorant). Shifted through 'coy, reserved', via 'scrupulous' to 'subtle' and now, as Neil Fitzgerald put it, 'sort of awright'.

4. **Silly** Not quite opposite, but close. Used to mean 'happy', then 'innocent, feeble' and now 'foolish'.

5. **Awful** Originally, inspiring awe.

6. **Egregious** Means outstandingly bad and used to mean outstandingly good. From Latin, 'standing out from the flock'.

7. **Wicked** Now a rather tame street-slang inversion.

8. **Fulsome** Still means cloying, insincere, for many of us, but often now used as a strong form of 'full', especially of praise.

9. **Bad** With thanks, or otherwise, to Michael Jackson.

10. **Presently** 'Used to mean right this minute and now means later because of the human tendency to put things off.' Della Mirandola.

A special bonus one, nominated by my friend Francis Wheen, who wrote to me as follows:

Wheen. You may not be familiar with it, but many of your readers in Scotland and Northern Ireland are. A Scottish (and Ulster) noun derived from the Old English hwǣne ('in some degree, somewhat, a little'), wheen began life meaning 'few, small amount', mostly in the phrase 'a wheen of...'

As the *OED* notes, however: 'A wheen (of), a few: in recent use = a 'good few', a fair number.' So when you hear a customer ask a fishmonger for 'a wheen of herring' (as I did in my Glaswegian childhood), he could mean either a few or a lot.

These days it's more likely to be the latter. See, for example, this tweet from the Scottish MEP Alyn Smith on 23 October 2013: 'Jings what a day! A wheen of votes, now legging it to Brussels and home ready to help out @theSNP campaign for Dunfermline MSP poll tomorrow.' Or this, from Ian Rankin, blogging on 12 November 2011: 'Signed a wheen of new books at No Alibis...' In most recent examples I can find in Scottish newspapers it clearly means 'a large number'.

Confusingly, however, dictionaries still lead with the old meaning. Here's the latest edition of *Chambers*, the greatest Scottish dictionary: 'a wheen 1. A few; 2: A good many.'

WORDS WITH OPPOSITE MEANINGS

Which brings us neatly to the next list, of words that have retained opposite meanings in contemporary English. Thanks to Stryker McGuire.

1. **Sanction** To approve or to disapprove.

2. **Oversight** To have responsibility for or to forget.

3. **Buckle** To do up or to collapse.

4. **Arguable** Can mean something that can be asserted or contradicted.

5. **Cleave** To split or to stick to. Apparently from different Old English roots.

6. **Dust** Can mean to remove dust or to apply it.

7. **Fast** Moving fast or stuck fast.

8. **Quite** Not much or absolutely.

9. **Qualified** Falling short or meeting requirements.

10. **Interesting** Meaning either an interesting or a stupid idea.

Finally, as Stewart Wood, Ed Miliband's shadow Cabinet adviser, said, 'Downhill from now on' can mean that the worst is over or still to come.

FICTIONAL VILLAINS

I caught up with the television series *Sherlock* only recently, and was struck by how unconvincing and un-sinister the character of Moriarty seemed. From my dim memory of the books, there wasn't much to him in Arthur Conan Doyle's original either. Here are some proper baddies …

1. **Charles Augustus Milverton** Martin Hoscik said the blackmailer in another Sherlock Holmes story, 'The Adventure of Charles Augustus Milverton', is more interesting than Moriarty.

2. **Count Olaf** *A Series of Unfortunate Events* by Lemony Snicket.

3. **Francis Urquhart** *House of Cards* by Michael Dobbs.

4. **Count Dracula** *Dracula* by Bram Stoker.

5. **Satan** From *Paradise Lost*, John Milton. John Blake nominated God in the same poem, but I rejected that as being too clever.

6. **Humbert Humbert** *Lolita* by Vladimir Nabokov.

7. **Long John Silver** *Treasure Island* by Robert Louis Stevenson. 'Them as dies'll be the lucky ones.'

8. **HAL** *2001: A Space Odyssey* written by Stanley Kubrick and Arthur C. Clarke.

9. **Phyllis Dietrichson** *Double Indemnity*, directed by Billy

Wilder. She is called Phyllis Nirdlinger in the original novella by James M. Cain.

10. Mrs Danvers *Rebecca* by Daphne du Maurier.

UPBEAT SONGS THAT TELL A SAD STORY

Rafael Behr, who was political editor of the *New Statesman*, asked if there were a word for 'uptempo, happy-sounding pop songs that actually tell a sad story', such as 'Up the Junction', by Squeeze. No, but I have a little list of examples.

1. **'Mrs Robinson'**, Simon and Garfunkel: Sounds like jaunty pop; tells a story of fear and alienation.

2. **'I Think I'm Gonna Kill Myself'**, Elton John.

3. **'Maxwell's Silver Hammer'**, the Beatles. A cheery little tune about a serial killer.

4. **'Don't Stop'**, Fleetwood Mac. About Christine McVie's separation from John McVie, Fleetwood Mac's bass guitarist.

5. **'Viva la Vida'**, Coldplay. Named after a painting by Frida Kahlo who had polio and a broken spine, and about her overcoming chronic pain. 'I always thought it was most bizarre to

use "Viva la Vida" when Ed Miliband won the Labour leadership,' said Jill Rutter.

6. **'She Called Up'**, Crowded House. 'A jaunty number about the suicide of their drummer,' according to Ben Stanley.

7. **'You're an Embarrassment'**, Madness. Written by Lee Thompson, the band's saxophone player, about the response of his wider family to the news of his teenage sister's pregnancy by a black man.

8. **'Girlfriend in a Coma'**, the Smiths. 'Has such a catchy tune,' said Sara Morris. 'The happiest sounding song about a dying partner that I can think of right now,' added Luke Hurst.

9. **'Five Get Over Excited'**, by the Housemartins. They were killed in a car crash, thrown into a river and poisoned. Possibly not in that order.

10. **'Positively 4th Street'**, Bob Dylan. 'Jangly folk-rock guitar juxtaposed with four minutes of lyrical vitriol.' Thanks to whoever runs the Cabot Learning Federation Government and Politics & Classical Civilisation Twitter account.

GENUINE SHOP NAMES

A letter in a Sunday newspaper recently contested the claim that Junk & Disorderly was the best punning shop name in Britain, claiming the title for a butcher in Tooting called Halal – Is It Meat You're Looking For. Sadly, there is no such shop. But these are all genuine.

1. **Wok This Way** Chinese take-away in Newcastle.

2. **Sun Tan Drews** Tanning salon, now closed, in north-east Fife university town.

3. **Curl Up and Dye** Hairdresser in many places, including Kingston.

4. **Melon Cauli** Greengrocer in Pheasey, Birmingham (the sign also says 'funeral work undertaken').

5. **Kumquat Mae** Vegetarian restaurant, Sheffield.

6. **Napoleon Boiler Parts** Alton, Hampshire. 'It almost makes us want our boiler to be repaired,' said Pauline and Bernard Sheridan.

7. **Lawn Order** Gardener's van.

8. **Sellfridges** A fridge shop in Stoke Newington, north London, recently closed.

9. **B-Side The C-Side** Record shop in Herne Bay.

10. **Maison D'Etre** Restaurant, Highbury Corner, north London.

This was a popular one, and so we went on:

11. Woksupp, Durham.

12. Jason Donervan, a Bristol kebab van.

13. Brighton Wok.

14. Style Counsel, hairdresser in Crewe.

15. Ali Barbers, Waltham Cross.

16. Oh My Cod! Chippy, Hertford.

17. Kung Food, Clerkenwell Road, London.

18. Bourne and Bread, sandwich shop at 26 Bourne Road, Colchester.

19. The Merchant of Tennis, Venice Beach, Los Angeles.

20. Tringfellows, Hertfordshire café.

21. Wright Hassall, Leamington solicitors.

22. Planet of the Grapes, wine shop chain in London.

23. The Codfather of Sole, chippy on Barry Island.

24. Fishcotheque, Waterloo.

25. Million Hair, Cardiff.

26. Crook and Blight, estate agent in Newport.

27. The Edinburgh Fringe, hairdresser in Edinburgh.

28. The Frock Exchange, second-hand clothes shop in Fulham Broadway.

29. R Daley Bread, bakery, Manchester.

30. Argue & Phibbs, solicitors, Sligo.

31. Harrison Ford, best car dealership in Ohio.

32. Tan Tropez, a tanning salon in Egham, apparently owned by former Fulham defender Rufus Brevett.

33. Past Caring, restoration firm in Cardiff.

34. Flaming Grate, fireplace installation firm, Cardiff. Nominated for its accidental sarcasm.

35. Amazing Grates, East Finchley.

36. The Batter of Bosworth, fish and chip shop near where Richard III was killed.

37. Doolittle and Dalley, Kidderminster estate agents.

38. Argee Bhajee, Oldham. Its slogan, 'Bringing the East End to the North', was choice, too.

39. Tanz'in'ere, Stalybridge.

40. Crops & Bobbers, hairdresser in Paddington.

41. La Cookshop, Durham. 'OK, so what we need is a name that sums up what we do, but also has a touch of European sophistication…' Jo Barrow imagined how it came about.

42. The Better Hearth, fireplace shop on Holloway Road.

43. Mr Resistor, lighting specialist, New Kings Road.

44. Salon Le Bon, hairdresser, Birmingham.

45. Karlsburgers, Cardiff.

46. Cooking: The Books, Cheltenham.

47. Fancy a Snack in the Mouth, Southampton Common fair.

48. Gelato Gusto, Artisan ice cream.

49. Mungo Deli, Knaresborough.

50. Typical Kebab, New Cross. Nominated by Jamie Thunder, who worried about its lack of ambition.

MIXED METAPHORS

'Mixed metaphors have been neglected in recent metaphor research,' according to an academic paper on artificial intelligence by the School of Computer Science at the University of Birmingham. So I am grateful to Anthony Polson for suggesting this collection.

1. 'Ahmadinejad wields axe to cement his position' *Independent* headline, 14 December 2010.

2. 'It would open up a can of worms and a legal minefield about freedom, religion and equalities legislation ... It may

open up old wounds and put people into the trenches; no one wants that.' David Burrowes, Conservative MP, on gay marriage, 17 January 2012.

3. 'He got the wrong end of the stick and started beating round the bush with it.' A mechanical and electrical consultant on a building site.

4. 'I don't like it. When you open that Pandora's box, you will find it full of Trojan horses.' Ernest Bevin, Labour Foreign Secretary, on the idea of a Council of Europe, 1948, quoted by Lord Strang, permanent under-secretary at the Foreign Office, in his memoir, *Home and Abroad*, 1956, p. 290.

5. 'I'm kickstarting a drive to get employee ownership into the bloodstream.' Nick Clegg, 17 January 2012.

6. 'Far-right vacuum could trigger "lone-wolf" attacks' *Independent* headline, 29 December 2012. Errors & Omissions editor Guy Keleny had some fun trying to imagine the precise mechanism involved.

7. 'They've put all their eggs in one basket and it's misfired.' Paul Merson, Sky football pundit, of West Ham's purchase of Andy Carroll.

8. 'Out of the hat on Monday night the Home Secretary produced the rabbit, the temporary provisions Bill, as her fig leaf to cover her major U-turn.' Simon Hughes, Lib Dem MP, 2008.

9. 'To take arms against a sea of troubles, / And by opposing end them.' Just to show that they are not always bad.

10. 'We're like the canary down the mine. We're the first people who pick up what's going on out there and what we're seeing at the moment is a boiling pot whose lid is coming off.'
    Markos Chrysostomou, Haringey Citizens Advice Bureau, on the effects of cuts, 19 November 2012.

Bonus track:

'Libyan revolutionary forces stormed through the streets of Sirte yesterday, tightening their noose on this last bastion of support for the fallen former leader, Muammar Gaddafi.' *Independent*, 12 October 2011. As Guy Keleny commented in his Errors & Omissions column: 'It would be possible to tighten a noose around a bastion, but nothing would be achieved by doing so.'

LOST POSITIVES

Jane Penson started this one off with ept and shevelled. 'When I was at boarding school, my friend and I spent hours in the school library with the *Oxford Dictionary* (twelve large dusty volumes) looking for them and we found lots,' she said. Here are my favourites.

1. **Placable** Last seen in Milton, according to Mark Wallace: 'Methought I saw him placable and mild.'

2. **Mantle** Lawrence Freedman. French *manteler*, fortify, from Latin *mantellum*, cloak.

3. **Dolent** From Latin *dolere*: to suffer or give pain.

4. **Traught** Distraught being a late Middle English form of distracted.

5. **Ert** Inert originally meant 'unskilled, inactive', from Latin *in-* (expressing negation) + *ars, art-* 'skill, art' (*Oxford Dictionary*).

6. **Gorm** Gormless was originally 'gaumless', from a dialect word, 'gaum', meaning 'understanding', from Old Norse *gaumr*, care, heed.

7. **Ruth** Tony Blair complained in his memoir that, far from being ruthless, he had 'plenty of ruth'.

8. **Gusted** Disgust comes from the Latin, *gustus*, taste.

9. **Plussed** Described by Karl Turner as 'the daddy of all lost positives.' 'Nonplussed' comes from the Latin *non plus*, not more; the noun originally meant 'a state in which no more can be said or done' (*Oxford Dictionary*).

10. **Chalant** Nonchalant comes from the French chaloir, concerned.

I ended up with so many lost positives that I could have compiled a small dictionary of them.

Here are another thirty-three, with thanks to Amaro Bhikkhu and others:

Advertent	Evitable	Pudent
Ane	Feck	Ravel
Beknownst	Flappable	Reck
Combobulated	Funct	Ruly
Corrigible	Gainly	Scrutable
Couth	Gruntled	Semble
Delible	Hap	Shevelled
Ebriated	Hinged	Sipid
Effable	List	Souciance, souciant
Ept	Mented	Racinated
Ertia	Parage	Turb

TAUTOLOGOUS ABBREVIATIONS

Thanks to Simmy Richman for suggesting that I should collect redundant words at the end of abbreviations, examples of what he calls RAS* syndrome. One correspondent proposed a list of a related phenomenon, of abbreviations that take longer to say than the words they stand for, such as VW, but there aren't ten of them.

1. **Please RSVP**

2. **RPG games** (Role-Playing Games)

3. **HIV virus**

---

* redundant acronym syndrome

4. **OPEC countries**

5. **LCD display**

6. **ISBN number**

7. **ABS brakes** (Anti-lock Braking System)

8. **PIN number**

9. **PAC code** (Port Authorisation Code, when changing provider but keeping same mobile phone number)

10. **ATM machine** Especially one belonging to TSB Bank.

EXAMPLES OF JOURNALESE

Romps, Tots and Boffins, by my friend Rob Hutton, is a guide to the strange language of news reporting. No sooner had the book gone to press than he noticed phrases that he had left out. These are called 'glaring omissions' in journalese, and here are ten of them, most of them contributed by Hutton himself.

1. **'A light-hearted sideways look'** As in: 'Newsman Robert Hutton has penned a light-hearted sideways look at the weird and wonderful world of the news.'

2. **'An area popular with joggers and dog-walkers'** Always the best place to hide a body.

3. **'Pen'** As a verb.

4. **'Brandish'** What referees do to red cards.

5. **'Silent killer'** Anything that might cause cancer in rats that doesn't make a noise. Nominated by Ms Person.

6. **'Frolicked'** What actresses do on beaches in full view of the photographers hiding in the bushes several hundred yards away.

7. **'Mercy dash'**

8. **'Purr-fect'** All cat-related news stories are required to contain this phrase by order of the independent press regulator working under the Royal Charter.

9. **'Wheelchair-bound'** Let's get rid of it.

10. **'Epidemic'** Of anything except actual diseases. Especially 'hidden epidemic'.

MOST INTERESTING POLITICIANS

I forgot to specify that I meant 'British' and 'active', so I am afraid I had to rule out some fine nominations. John Stonehouse, for example, the Czech spy and Labour MP for Walsall North who disappeared to Australia in 1974 having staged his own death, would have been a candidate.

1. **Ed Balls** Quad-core intellectual processor who was Gordon Brown's spare brain capacity for sixteen years; a better economist than his rival, George Osbourne.

2. **Andrew Adonis** With academies and HS2 (even if it never happens), Lord Adonis has achieved more than all but a handful of elected ministers.

3. **David Cameron** Too easily dismissed as a privileged smoothie, he is an instinctive politician and fitfully ambitious thinker.

4. **Stella Creasy** Talks so fast and is so busy on Twitter it's easy to overlook how deeply she is steeped in Labour history and political and psychological theory.

5. **Michael Gove** Once a fierce Thatcherite, his conversion to advocate of comprehensive excellence for poor pupils was a lasting Blairite gain.

6. **David Laws** The only Lib Dem on the list. Shone brightly in his seventeen days in the Cabinet in 2010. The job in the City before politics lends some depth.

7. **Boris Johnson** The combination buffoon and polymath is sufficiently dazzling to obscure a thin record as London mayor.

8. **Grant Shapps** It's unusual to have a front-rank politician who has traded under an assumed name (writing books such as *How to Bounce Back from Recession* under the pseudonym Michael Green).

9. **Nicola Sturgeon** After long being seen as an extra in Alex

Salmond's film, turned out to have a mind of her own: insisted on a simple Yes-No referendum on Scottish independence.

10. **Anna Soubry** Deserves our lasting gratitude for banning civil-service jargon as health minister.

SPOONERISMS

'She was so beautiful that the two sisty uglers didn't cinderise Recognella.' I am grateful to Michael Fishberg for drawing to my attention a 1962 recording of 'Cinderella', written by Jack Ross and Elmer Nemeth, in which Ross tells the story in spoonerisms. I think we should use them more. Lecund sowest hulme of former, indeed.

1. **Mare in handage** The prandsome hince was just about to ask for Cinderella's when the strock clarted to trike swelve.

2. **Plaster man**

3. **Porter logged witches**

4. **We'll have the hags flung out** Philip Ardagh, from his *Book of Howlers, Blunders and Random Mistakery*.

5. **Mean as custard**

6. **Flow snurries**

7. **Lloyd Fraud** Chris Bryant, the Labour MP, made a Freudian

slip when he referred to the Work and Pensions minister, Lord Freud.

8. **Shake a tower**

9. **'The Lord is a shoving leopard'** Attributed to William Spooner, warden of New College, Oxford, 1903–1924, but probably made up by one of his students.

10. **The weight of rages** One of only two authenticated Spoonerisms uttered by Spooner himself. The other is 'The Kinquering Congs their Titles Take'.

Also nominated: 'Ache and Stale Pie'; My parents are 'Dumb and Mad'; 'Cone Fall'; Log on to 'Dr Kinlay's Facebook'; Time to watch the 'Snort Spews'.

TAUTOLOGIES

There is a pub on Borough High Street, just south of London Bridge, called The Barrowboy and Banker, which ought to be the secret HQ of the internet campaign called Tautologywatch, run by Amol Rajan, editor of the *Independent*. To curry favour with him, I offer this list.

1. **Null and void**

2. **'*Moments in Time*'** Title of the BBC's review of 2013.

3. **Free gift**

4. **Pre-planned** and **forward planning**

5. **Work colleague**

6. **Safe haven**

7. **Advance warning** and **advance notice**

8. **Past history**

9. **Loose change**

10. **Deliberately targeted**

And the next twenty:

11. Pick and choose

12. Raze to the ground

13. General consensus

14. Forward not back. Labour election slogan, 2005.

15. Brief sojourn. Sojourn means 'temporary stay', from late Latin, day trip, *sub+diurnum*, less than a day.

16. Wholly unnecessary

17. Meaningless guff

18. Deliberate lie

19. Added bonus

20. Last vestige

21. General public. This was nominated by Ramesh Biswas, who also suggested *The Color Purple*, although this is technically a pleonasm, 'the use of more words than are necessary to convey meaning'.

22. Time and tide wait(s) for no man. Was originally a tautology, in that tide is a synonym for time, before it evolved into what sounds like a Canute-like proverb.

23. Strait and narrow. Usually rendered as 'straight and narrow', which is a misquotation of the Bible, Matthew 7:14: 'Strait is the gate, and narrow is the way which leadeth unto life, and few there be that find it' (strait means narrow).

24. Few in number

25. Short in stature

26. A first introduction

27. Harbinger of things to come

28. Self-confessed

29. 'The Deadly Assassin', a classic *Doctor Who* episode.

30. Mutual consent

TRANSLATED TAUTOLOGIES

1. **Naan** means bread.

2. **Sahara** means desert.

3. **Kalahari** also means desert.

4. **Sharia** means law.

5. **Avon** means river.

6. **La Brea** means the Tar. So The La Brea Tar Pits in Los Angeles are 'The The Tar Tar Pits'.

7. **Mere** means lake, so Lake Windermere means Lake Winder Lake.

8. **Tahoe** also means lake in the Washo language of Native Americans.

9. **Astana**, the capital of Kazakhstan, means 'capital' in Kazakh.

10. **Torpenhow Hill** in Cumbria is sometimes said to mean Hillhillhill Hill, but that etymology (tor, pen and how are Old English, Welsh and Danish respectively) is doubtful.

But I haven't listed 'hoi polloi', ancient Greek for 'the common people', because people who point out that 'the hoi polloi' means 'the the common people' are a bit irritating.

SONGS THAT MEAN THE OPPOSITE OF WHAT MOST PEOPLE THINK

This started when Peter Watt said that he was traumatised, because he had just discovered that Tom Jones's 'Delilah' is about a vengeful murder. Damian Counsell pointed out that there are many more examples, and he was right.

1. **'Every Breath You Take'**, the Police, is about stalking.

2. **'You're Gorgeous'**, Baby Bird, is about a dirty old man.

3. **'The Future's So Bright'**, Timbuk3, is about nuclear war.

4. **'The One I Love'**, REM, is about using people.

5. **'The Drugs Don't Work'**, the Verve. 'It's about Richard Ashcroft's dying dad not Britpop indulgence,' according to Jem Stone.

6. **'Born in the USA'**, Bruce Springsteen. 'Classically misunderstood by the Reagan camp,' said Giles Coren. The most popular nomination for this list: a bitter criticism of modern America often mistaken for a patriotic anthem.

7. **'I Believe in Father Christmas'**, Greg Lake. Protest against commercialisation.

8. **'Part of the Union'**, Strawbs. Sarcastic anti-union song.

9. **'Rockin' in the Free World'**, in which Neil Young castigates rockers for ignoring social problems. East Europeans took it up as a pro-west, pro-democracy anthem.

10. '**Happy Together**', the Turtles. He thinks about her day and night but has never even spoken to her.

Also nominated:

11. 'In the Summertime', by Mungo Jerry, 'as it's about drink driving and date rape', said Stella Creasy MP.

12. 'Young Girl', by Gary Puckett and the Union Gap, about underage sex with older man.

13. 'I Don't Like Mondays', the Boomtown Rats, which is about a school shooting, not the start of the working week, James Chapman pointed out.

14. 'No Woman No Cry', Bob Marley. Many think it means you only cry if you're in love; actually it's telling a woman not to be upset. David Aaronovitch added: In my sometimes lovelorn early 20s I thought it meant, 'I haven't got a woman and I'm trying not to cry.' Sarah Churchwell said: When I first heard it I thought it was 'No Woman No Crime'. But that's getting on to another long, long list, of misheard lyrics.

15. 'Jerusalem', words by William Blake, has to be the daddy of all of these, said Rob Davies. I'm not so sure. Nobody knows what the obscurantist poem means, so most people cannot think it means the opposite. All we know is that it is the official anthem of the 'Questions To Which The Answer Is No' cult.

16. 'Rainy Day Women #12 & 35', Bob Dylan. Hippy anthem with a repeated line telling everyone to get stoned that was actually about how boring stoners are. So I am told.

17. '99 Red Balloons', Nena. The song ends with them drifting across a post-nuclear-war world. I didn't know that it was a protest song, but apparently lots of people do.

18. 'Lucy in the Sky With Diamonds', Beatles ('it really isn't about drugs', says William French), and 'Perfect Day', Lou Reed ('it is').

19. 'On The Good Ship Lollipop', Shirley Temple: the ship is actually an aircraft, a Douglas DC-2.

20. 'I Will Always Love You', Dolly Parton. A wedding reception favourite even though it's about a break-up.

UNEXPECTED ETYMOLOGIES

A discussion in the office about whether certain words – feisty, blowsy, bubbly – were sexist because they were almost always applied to women degenerated into a trawl through the *Oxford Dictionary* for the surprising origins of some words.

1. **Gerrymander** A new voting district in Massachusetts in the shape of a salamander favoured Governor Elbridge Gerry's party.

2. **Blowsy** Early 17th century: from obsolete blowze, 'beggar's female companion'.

3. **Bumf** Late 19th century: abbreviation of slang bum-fodder.

4. **Humble pie** A pun on 'umbles', offal, considered to be inferior food.

5. **Raspberry (To blow a)** Raspberry tart, rhyming slang for 'fart'.

6. **Tawdry** Early 17th century: short for tawdry lace, contraction of St Audrey's lace, after patron saint of Ely, where cheap finery was sold at a fair.

7. **Shibboleth** From Hebrew for 'ear of corn', used (in the Bible) as a test of nationality by its difficult pronunciation.

8. **Prurient** Late 16th century: mental itching, from Latin for 'itching, longing'.

9. **Feisty** Late 19th century: from earlier feist, fist, 'small dog', from fisting or hound, a derogatory term for a lapdog, from Middle English fist, 'break wind'.

10. **Shambles** Originally a butcher's slaughterhouse.

Also nominated:

11. Laconic. Refers to the characteristic humour of the Greek region of Laconia, the capital of which was Sparta. The best example of which was when Philip of Macedon laid siege to Laconia, as recounted by Plutarch: 'When Philip wrote thus to the Spartans: "If once I enter into your territories, I will destroy ye all, never to rise again"; they answered him with the single word, "If."'

12. Blurb. Named after Miss Belinda Blurb, a fictional endorser created by Gelett Burgess, an American wit, in 1907.

13. Effete. Originally meant worn out by bearing young.

14. Jejune. Originally fasting, barren.

15. Nondescript. The *Oxford Dictionary* says 'late 17th century: in the sense "not previously described or identified scientifically"', which is not a sense in which it is used today.

MOST ENGLISH REMARKS OF ALL TIME

Boris Johnson once said of his Anglican belief: 'My faith is a bit like Magic FM in the Chilterns, in that the signal comes and goes.' A lot of people, including David Cameron who likes to quote it, have been very taken by this most English of sentiments. So I asked for other candidates.

1. **'I am just going outside and may be some time.'** Captain Oates.

2. **'I think it's easing.'** (Of the rain.)

3. **'Old maids hiking to Holy Communion through the mists of the autumn morning.'** George Orwell, 'England Your England'. Often misquoted as 'biking' to Holy Communion, and even, by another very English prime minister, John Major, as 'bicycling'.

4. **'Who you looking at, mate?'** Nominated by Sean Kenny. 'Usually as spoken in a pub, in a market town, on a Saturday night. But can be used any time.'

5. **'Sorry.'**

6. **'By God, sir, I've lost my leg!' 'By God, sir, so you have!'** Lord Uxbridge and the Duke of Wellington at the battle of Waterloo.

7. **'Why don't you fall into two very lovely lines?'** Sergeant Wilson, *Dad's Army*.

8. **'Well, you know me, I ain't one to gossip.'** Dot Cotton, *EastEnders*.

9. **'It looked a tad sticky at Dunkirk.'** Eddie Cozens, nominated by his grandson Mark Wallace, who had asked, 'Did you ever think we might lose the war?'

10. **'Crashed slow-rolling near the ground. Bad show.'** Douglas Bader's logbook, on the accident that cost him his legs.

MISUSED FABLES

Every time a footballer or football manager talks about 'sour grapes', Jerry Campbell wants to shout at the television. 'Has nobody read Aesop's fables?' he asked. 'It does not just mean complaining. It means pretending the prize just lost was not worth winning to avoid admitting disappointment.'

1. **Sour grapes** Not another way of saying 'whinge'.

2. **Pyrrhic victory** A victory won at too great a cost, not just an empty victory.

3. **Midas touch** It was a curse.

4. **Canute** He sat in the waves to show sycophantic courtiers that he was powerless to hold back the tide.

5. **Break the mould** It means something is uniquely beautiful, not that it is a dramatic change. From 'The Frenzy of Orlando' by Ludovico Ariosto: 'Nature made him, and then broke the mould.'

6. **The Good Samaritan** 'Unless you have anti-Samaritan prejudice, it's hard to get the point,' noted Colin Rosenthal.

7. **The writing on the wall** Usually used to mean an obvious sign that everyone can see. In the Bible it is a hidden warning. No one but Daniel could understand this cryptic message of doom.

8. **Devil's advocate** Not the taker of a position for the sake of

argument (that's a troll), but someone who puts the devil's claims to candidates for sainthood.

9. **Frankenstein** Not to be confused with his monster.

10. **Meritocracy** A parable set in 2033, published in 1958, by Michael Young. It was a bad thing.

PALINDROMES

If I ask for palindromes I don't get just palindromes. I get a Cabinet Minister with a palindromic name – Lord Glenelg, Whig Secretary of State for War and the Colonies, 1835–1839 – nominated by the wonderful Labour History Group.

1. **Was it a car or a cat I saw?**

2. **Satan oscillate my metallic sonatas** Devised by Stephen Fry.

3. **Revered now, I live on. O did I do no evil, I wonder, ever?**

4. **A man, a plan, a canal: Panama!**

5. **Dog, as a devil deified, lived as a God**

6. **Able was I ere I saw Elba**

7. **It's Ade, Cilla, Sue, Dame Vita, Edna, Nino, Emo! Come on in and eat; I've made us all iced asti.**

8. **Dammit I'm mad!**

9. **Rise to vote sir**

10. **'SOS'** by **Abba** Rare example of a hit single where both song and artist are palindromes.

And the bonus eleventh:

11. Straw? No, too stupid a fad. I put soot on warts

Samuel Hudson warned that too many of these might trigger an attack of 'aibohphobia'.

WORDS USED ONLY WITH ONE OTHER WORD

Stewart Wood, shadow minister without portfolio, asked about obsolete words that survive only in idiomatic phrases, and contributed two. It was impossible to keep this list to the usual limit, so this is a top twenty:

1. Fettle

2. Figment

3. Serried

4. Unsung

5. **Amok**. As Woody Allen once said, 'If you're tired, we can walk amok.'

6. **Hale**

7. **Fledged**

8. **Shrift**

9. **Clarion**

10. **Dulcet**

11. **Dudgeon**

12. **Halcyon**

13. **Squib**

14. **Shebang**

15. **Bated**

16. **Swingeing**

17. **Scot**

18. **Inclement**

19. **Knell**

20. **Batten**

ENGLISH MONARCHS 1066–1707

Sir Michael Barber, who was head of the Prime Minister's Delivery Unit from 2001 to 2005, suggested this list: monarchs of England 'judged on leaving the country in better shape than they found it', and he provided most of the rankings here:

1. **Henry VII** Michael Barber's top choice.

2. **William I** I, for one, welcome our new Norman overlords.

3. **Elizabeth I** 'For declining to make windows into men's souls,' said Michael McCarthy.

4. **Edward III** 'Crécy. Black Prince. Bicameral parliament. Treason Act. English used in law. JPs.' David Head.

5. **Henry II** 'Juries, rule of law.' Louise McCudden.

6. **William III and Mary II** Bill of Rights.

7. **Henry V** Agincourt.

8. **Harold II Godwinson** 'Defeat of Harald Hardrada meant there was a united kingdom of England for William to inherit.' John Blake.

9. **Edward II** 'For losing at Bannockburn and thus ensuring 1707 would be a Union not an incorporation.' Alex Massie.

10. **John** 'For being rubbish, thus giving rise to the Magna Carta,' said Ian Silvera.

UNISEX NAMES OF MPS

When Cara Hilton won a Scottish Parliament by-election, David Mills asked whether there had ever been an MP called Cara. The Labour History Group said no, but there had been a Carol, who was a man. Thus this list was born.

1. **Ray Michie** Female, Liberal Democrat, 1987–2001.

2. **Robin Cook** Male, Labour, 1974–2005.

3. **Carol Mather** Male, Conservative, 1970–1987. A soldier who said of Douglas Hurd's German-style coat, 'Last time I saw anyone wearing a coat like that, I shot him.'

4. **Mervyn Pike** Female, Conservative, 1956–1974, after which she became chairman of the Women's Royal Voluntary Reserve.

5. **Meredith Titterington** Male, Labour, 1945–1949.

6. **Evelyn Emmet** Female, Conservative, 1955–1965. Unlike Evelyns King (Labour, 1945–1950, then Conservative, 1964–1979) and Walkden (Labour, 1941–1950), who were male.

7. **Beverley Baxter** Male, Conservative, 1935–1964, who had previously been editor of the *Daily Express*, 1929–1933.

8. **Hilary Benn** Male, Labour, since 1999. He and **Kerry McCarthy**, female, Labour, since 2005, are the two current MPs.

9. **Hyacinth Morgan** Male, Labour, 1929–1931 and 1940–1955.

10. **Jocelyn Cadbury** Male, Conservative, 1979–1982.

WAYS OF DEFEATING THE DALEKS

'There's a problem with the Daleks,' said Steven Moffat, producer of *Doctor Who*. 'They have been defeated by the Doctor about four hundred times. Surely they should just see the Tardis approaching, say, "Oh, it's him," and trudge away.' Here, thanks to Cavan Scott and Mark Wright (*Who-ology*), are just a few of their weaknesses responsible for just ten of those four hundred defeats in the programme's fifty-year history.

1. Stick mud in the Dalek's eye and push it over a cape to insulate it from its power supply. First and best method.

2. Dig a hole in the desert, cover it with an old cardigan, get a Dalek to chase you and hope it falls in.

3. Leave a cooling duct open. If you're lucky, a burst of ice will engulf passing Daleks at just the right moment.

4. Blast it with a directional ultrasonic beam of rock'n'roll.

5. Push it into a mirrored corridor. It will be exterminated by its own ricocheting death ray.

6. Topple it out of a third-storey warehouse door.

7. If you are Davros, modify the Movellan virus to eradicate your own creations. But make sure you are not susceptible to the plague yourself. Whoops.

8. Get it to make a mistake. Some Daleks are so self-critical that they'll overreact and self-destruct.

9. Get it to absorb human DNA. It will question its own existence and exterminate itself.

10. Stare into the heart of the Tardis, giving you the power to delete the Daleks from history. The downside is you start to die. Upside is the Doctor kisses you, absorbs the power and regenerates.

ANAGRAMS

Mary Ann Sieghart, a former columnist on the *Independent on Sunday*, found a London Underground map on the internet on which all the station names were replaced with anagrams, which gave me the first on this list.

1. **Kensington High Street** Togetherness thinking.

2. **Eleven plus two** Twelve plus one. Spooky.

3. **Manchester City** Synthetic cream.

4. **New York Times** Monkeys write.

5. **Public relations** Crap built on lies. Attributed to Mick Tully, 2001.

6. **Houses of Parliament** Shameful operations.

7. **Anagram** If you type it into Google, it asks 'did you mean nag a ram'.

8. **Alec Guinness** Genuine class.

9. **Proust** Stupor.

10. **Cameron** Romance. Pointed out to me by a taxi driver, to explain his prediction that the Conservative leader would win the 2010 election.

MOST BEAUTIFUL BRITISH RAILWAY JOURNEYS

Andrew Adonis asked, on his way to the Cheltenham Literary Festival: 'Is the North Cotswold Line – Kemble, Stroud etc – the most beautiful in England?' He said it was 'on a short shortlist', so I asked readers to help me compile the rest, including the rest of the UK.

1. East Coast Main Line. The view of Durham is prized, but many vote for the 'glorious' stretch from **Newcastle to Edinburgh**, especially Alnmouth to Berwick when the tide is in.

2. **Edinburgh to Aberdeen** Continuing northwards, 'none can compete with the Forth and Tay bridges', according to Bob Reid.

3. **Settle to Carlisle** Especially the Ribblehead viaduct.

4. **Barking to Gospel Oak** on the London Overground. 'This journey looks at the urban landscape, but not the showy, award-winning portion,' said Paul T. Horgan. Fine new rolling stock, too.

5. **Cambrian Coast Line** in West Wales.

6. **Hope Valley** in Derbyshire.

7. **West Highland Line** from Mallaig to Oban in Scotland.

8. **North Cotswold Line** Andrew Adonis's favourite.

9. **Carstairs to Lockerbie** on the West Coast Line.

10. **Taunton to Penzance** Including Brunel's Royal Albert Bridge at Saltash and the Dawlish coast, now repaired.

NEW CLICHÉS THAT SHOULD BE BANNED

I have written a whole book, *The Banned List*, in an attempt to fight meaningless verbiage and over-familiar phrases. Yet new horrors are constantly invented and then repeated. Here are ten recent examples, many of them nominated by my friend Magda Sachs.

1. **Built environment** Means buildings.

2. **Piece of work** As in, 'I am doing a piece of work around troubled families.' ('Around', used to mean 'about', was banned long ago.)

3. **Vision and visioning** As in, 'What is your vision for this piece of work?' and 'We are visioning the piece of work.'

4. **Embedded** Never needed.

5. **Talking in the present tense about past events** As in, 'Richard the Third then moves his army to the north …'

6. **Wrap-around** To describe anything other than packaging.

7. **Innocent children** As opposed to complicit children, about whom we are indifferent.

8. **Sneak preview** It's invariably just a preview. Worse is 'sneak peek'. And worst of all is 'sneak peak'.

9. **Future-proof** Time machines are not real.

10. **Stand idly by** Anyone really idle would sit down.

PHRASES THAT OUGHT TO BE OFF THE MENU

Such was my success in banning things that Matthew Beardmore-Gray suggested that I should take the censor's pen to pretentious descriptions on menus.

1. Anything that mentions '**foam**'.

2. **Slow-cooked** Meaning cooked elsewhere and reheated.

3. Vegetables '**nestling**' with each other. Often in a '**bed**'.

4. **Jus** Nominated by Sadie Smith who insisted it's gravy.

5. **Sourced** Suggested by John West (no, really), especially ethically or locally.

6. **Drizzle** Usually means drip.

7. **Hand-carved** Not carved by robots.

8. **Vine-ripened heritage tomatoes** Still taste of nothing.

9. **Artisanal breads** Produced by medieval guilds.

10. **Coulis** Means a sauce of dubious sugary origin.

WORDS THAT OUGHT TO BE USED MORE OFTEN

One of my friends has a habit of announcing, out of the blue, his word of the day. Once it was poltroon. This prompted me to think of all those words that ought to be rescued from the penumbra of obscurity. After all, having railed against cliché at such length, I ought to offer up some words that are not familiar enough to be used instead.

1. **Stramash** Fight, uproar. Scottish and northern English.

2. **Seldom** In decline, according to Google Ngram, which tracks the number of times words are used in books, since 1950. Feels similar to 'splendid', although that declined most sharply after 1920.

3. **Inchoate** 'Just begun and so not fully formed or developed,' says the Oxford Dictionary.

4. **Badinage** Much better word than 'banter'. Nominated by someone calling themselves 'Bolly Knickers', which is a form of it, I suppose.

5. **Insouciance** 'Casual lack of concern,' from the French for 'not worrying'.

6. **Putative** A surprisingly new word, becoming popular in the 1970s, according to Google.

7. **Thrice** It must be the sound, because 'trice' was also nominated.

8. **Boondoggle** 'An unnecessary, wasteful, or fraudulent project.' Also a verb.

9. **Mellifluous** From the Latin for honey and flow. 'It's so onomatopoeic,' said Jessica Elgot.

10. **Peripatetic** 'Travelling from place to place.'

Whenever I am criticised for wanting to reduce all communication to clicks and grunts, just because I want to ban a few hundred clichés, I point out that the English language is infinitely rich. No matter how many words I ban there will be thousands of more interesting ones to take their place. And so it proved, because many, many more marvellous words were nominated for this list:

Bathos	Garrulous	Persiflage
Bletherskite	Gawkish	Prolix
Brouhaha	Gobbledygook	Quixotic
Bucolic	Hogwhimpering	Rumpus
Crepuscular	Irksome	Sedulous
Dandy	Malingerer	Skulduggery
Desultory	Mithering	Trifle
Dolt	Mouldering	Unctuous
Ensconced	Nugatory	Whiffling
Frippery	Panjandrum	Winsome

PARTY CONFERENCE SPEECHES

I didn't specify leaders' speeches, so I have included notable oratory from would-be leaders, a deputy leader and, in Bill Clinton's case, a visitor.

1. **Hugh Gaitskell, 1960** 'There are some of us who will fight, and fight, and fight again, to save the party we love.'

2. **Harold Wilson, 1963** 'The Britain that is going to be forged in the white heat of this revolution will be no place for restrictive practices.'

3. **Michael Heseltine, 1976** On Labour: 'A one-legged army: Left! Left! Left!'

4. **Norman Tebbit, 1981** On his unemployed father: 'He didn't riot; he got on his bike and looked for work.'

5. **Margaret Thatcher, 1984** Eleven hours after the Brighton bomb that morning. Braver than 'the Lady's not for turning' in 1981.

6. **Neil Kinnock, 1985** 'I'll tell you what happens with impossible promises. You start with far-fetched resolutions. They are then pickled into a rigid dogma, a code, and you go through the years sticking to that, out-dated, misplaced, irrelevant to the real needs, and you end in the grotesque chaos of a Labour council – a *Labour* council – hiring taxis to scuttle round a city handing out redundancy notices to its own workers.'

7. **John Prescott, 1993** Helped to win the vote on one member, one vote for John Smith: 'This man, our leader, has put his head on the block.'

8. **Bill Clinton, 2002** 'Clinton, Bill, Arkansas CLP, New Labour.'

9. **David Cameron, 2005** Blew away leadership rival David Davis with a 'walk and talk'. No one remembers what he actually said, though.

10. **Tony Blair, 2006** His farewell speech in which he thanked his wife, Cherie: 'At least I don't have to worry about her running off with the bloke next door.'

GREAT BANDS WITH TERRIBLE NAMES

We have to start on this list, as Tom Doran suggested, by considering the Beatles, 'as it's just a rubbish pun'. Beat, Beatles, see? Although that would suppose that the Beatles were a great band. This list was a hotly contested, highly subjective affair. A bit like many words, if you look at band names long enough, you realise how peculiar they have been all along.

1. **Humble Pie** 'Steve Marriott's post-Small Faces band. Epically awful name; reminds me of Creme Brulée, which was Les McQueen's former band in *The League of Gentlemen*,' said Tom Doran.

2. **Oasis**

3. **The Jesus and Mary Chain**

4. **Echo and the Bunnymen**

5. **Mott the Hoople** Mind you, the band was called Silence before that.

6. **Teenage Fanclub** 'I've got all the T-shirts, but boy am I ashamed to wear them,' said Stuart Ritchie.

7. **Joy Division** Not my thing, but people like them and I've always thought it an unusually daft name.

8. **Supertramp** Taken from the title of a book by W. H. Davies, *The Autobiography of a Super-Tramp*.

9. **Coldplay** Anyone know why?

10. **Led Zeppelin** As Peter A Russell said, 'When you think of it…'

FILMS PANNED AS TURKEYS THAT ARE ACTUALLY QUITE GOOD

Here is an idea I borrowed from Richard T. Kelly's book of alternative movie lists, called *Ten Bad Dates with De Niro*, which includes 'Ten so-called turkeys that are actually terrific'. As he said: 'The game is best played with movies that remain generally dismissed as piss-poor.' My fellow film critics have added to and updated his list.

1. *Sorcerer*, 1977. Richard T. Kelly: 'A terrific picture in which William Friedkin laid down a template for the future of music video.'

2. *1941*, 1979. Pete Hoskin: 'Far from being one of Spielberg's worst films, it's one of his best.'

3. *One from the Heart*, 1982. Richard T. Kelly: 'The film went $11m over budget before it tanked with audiences and Francis Ford Coppola wondered if it was worth it. It was, maestro, it was.'

4. *The King of Comedy*, 1983. Gabriel Milland: 'Wonderful final scene and great performances from three leads.'

5. *Red Dawn*, 1984. Alex Massie: 'The apotheosis of Reagan-era Cold War ass-kicking. Shamefully under-appreciated.'

6. *Ishtar*, 1987. Richard T. Kelly: 'This colossal commercial failure, funnily enough, is a heartening comedy about failure.'

7. *The Adventures of Baron Munchausen*, 1988. Lee Ravitz: 'Terry Gilliam's visual masterpiece', but it cost $47m to make and earnt only $8m at the box office.

8. *The Hudsucker Proxy*, 1994. Joe H.: 'A delightful and hilarious pastiche of the rapid-fire Hollywood classics from the 1940s and 1950s.'

9. *Mary Reilly*, 1996. Richard T. Kelly: 'A Jekyll and Hyde movie comes along every year, but this is the only one to conjure the third person enigma of Stevenson's classic.'

10. *The Big Lebowski*, 1998. Borderline. Hardly a turkey but, as Larry Ryan said, 'Considered a bit of a dud at the time – and it's obviously The Greatest.'

POLITICAL MYTHS

How people believe what they want to …

1. 'It was treachery with a smile on its face.' Margaret Thatcher blamed her fall on a disloyal Cabinet. Not so: backbench Tories did her in because the Poll Tax would have cost them their seats.

2. 'They're all the same.' This comment, about politicians or political parties, is the most tedious reflex of conventional wisdom, as my friend Tom Doran pointed out. It is not true, and if you really think it is, vote UKIP (or whatever).

3. Tony Blair claimed to have seen Jackie Milburn play at Newcastle, when the player had retired before the Blair family arrived from Australia. An oft-repeated misunderstanding. What Blair said on BBC radio was that he 'came just after Jackie Milburn'.

4. There was a 'sea change' said James Callaghan in 1979, 'and it is for Mrs Thatcher'. But that was just an excuse. If he had gone to the polls in 1978, Labour could have held on.

5. 'Petrol prices go up but they never go down.' The implication is that oil companies are stealthily and always increasing their profit margins by failing to reflect falls in world oil prices as quickly as they pass on price rises. The Office of Fair Trading has produced graphs that show it ain't so.

6. Memory of a goldfish. A metaphor often used in politics that's wrong. Goldfish can be trained to push levers to obtain food,

says David Bradley in his book, *Deceived Wisdom*. Nor do ostriches bury their heads in sand.

7. The post-war Liberal-Conservative coalition was brought down by the Tory backbench 1922 Committee. The Committee was formed in 1923 by Tory MPs elected after the coalition's fall.

8. Left-wing Labour councils discouraged competitive sports in schools in the 1980s. Conor Ryan, who was schools press officer for the Labour-controlled Inner London Education Authority at the time, wrote:

> I organised the launch of a detailed independent research report on team games in London schools, accompanied by great photos of scores of London school sporting success stories, disproving the idea that the ILEA – and not a few misguided heads – was anti-competitive sport. It won plaudits from the *Mail* and *Telegraph* at the time! The Labour political leadership of the ILEA in 1988 was keen to promote it in London schools.

9. 'The rich get richer and the poor get poorer.' It was true in the 1990s, but the degree of wealth inequality in Britain has stayed roughly the same since then, whatever Thomas Piketty says.

10. 'Too early to say' what the impact of the French Revolution was: Chinese premier Zhou Enlai misunderstood in 1971. He thought he was being asked about the student riots three years before.

ORIGINAL TITLES OF NOVELS

Very few great novels would have been better with their early titles. I should report, though, that some people did not take this list seriously. The original title of *The Very Hungry Caterpillar* was not *Murder at Midnight*, Michael Deacon. Nor, Tom Chivers, was *Wuthering Heights* going to be called *Captain Zapstar and the Death-Robots of Omnicron 19*.

1. **The Man of Feeling** *Lucky Jim*, by Kingsley Amis.

2. **Strangers from Within** In the care of Faber editor Charles Monteith, William Golding's novel emerged as *Lord of the Flies*, according to Faber editor Richard T. Kelly.

3. **Pop, girls, etc.** The working title of *High Fidelity*, by Nick Hornby.

4. **Catch-18** The first chapter of my favourite novel was published in a magazine under this title, but it clashed with Leon Uris's *Mila 18*.

5. **The Last Man in Europe** A lot of nominations for *Nineteen Eighty-Four*.

6. **Trimalchio in West Egg** One of many horrible titles dithered over by F. Scott Fitzgerald before he decided on *The Great Gatsby*.

7. **The Kingdom by the Sea** *Lolita*, by Vladimir Nabokov.

8. **The Ends of the Earth** The title of Douglas Adams's proposal

for a radio series, which was originally called 'Fits'. It ended up as *The Hitchhiker's Guide to the Galaxy*.

9. **The Dead Undead** Several nominations, including from David Tuck, for the working title of Bram Stoker's book, which became *The Undead* and then *Dracula*.

10. **Tomorrow is Another Day** Margaret Mitchell was just going to use the last line of *Gone With the Wind*.

11. And finally, it is not a novel despite containing elements of fiction, but *Four-and-a-Half Years of Struggle Against Lies, Stupidity and Cowardice* was published as *Mein Kampf*.

DOUGLAS ADAMS QUOTATIONS

Everyone knows that 42 is the Answer to the Ultimate Question of Life, the Universe and Everything. But Douglas Adams gave us many more memorable sayings, in the *Hitchhiker's Guide to the Galaxy* series, *Dirk Gently's Holistic Detective Agency*, scripts for *Doctor Who* and elsewhere. Here are ten of the best.

1. 'I love deadlines. I love the whooshing noise they make as they go by.' *The Salmon of Doubt*.

2. 'If you try and take a cat apart to see how it works, the first thing you have on your hands is a non-working cat.' *The Salmon of Doubt*.

3. 'He felt that his whole life was some kind of dream and he sometimes wondered whose it was and whether they were enjoying it.' *The Hitchhiker's Guide to the Galaxy*.

4. 'Ford! There's an infinite number of monkeys outside who want to talk to us about this script for *Hamlet* they've worked out.' *The Hitchhiker's Guide to the Galaxy*.

5. On asking for directions: 'My own strategy is to find a car … which looks as if it knows where it's going and follow it.' *The Long Dark Tea-Time of the Soul*.

6. 'The seat received him in a loose and distant kind of way, like an aunt who disapproves of the last fifteen years of your life.' *Dirk Gently's Holistic Detective Agency*.

7. 'Blackness swims toward you like a school of eels who have just seen something that eels like a lot.' *Hitchhiker's Guide to the Galaxy* text adventure game 1985.

8. 'A learning experience is one of those things that say, "You know that thing you just did? Don't do that."' An interview in the *Daily Nexus* in 2000, reprinted in *The Salmon of Doubt*.

9. '"Life," said Marvin dolefully, "loathe it or ignore it, you can't like it."' Even better than Marvin the Paranoid Android's better-known line: 'Life? Don't talk to me about life.' *The Hitchhiker's Guide to the Galaxy*.

10. 'Clixby (adjective): Politely rude. Briskly vague. Firmly uninformative.' *The Meaning of Liff*, co-written with John Lloyd.

QUESTIONS TO WHICH THE ANSWER IS NO

I have a strange hobby: collecting headlines in the form of questions to which the author or publisher implies that the answer is yes when anyone with any sense knows it is not. I published a book of these (*Questions To Which The Answer Is No*) in 2012 but continued to compile them: here are ten more that I have collected since.

1. **Is China more democratic than the West?** Martin Jacques, *BBC News Magazine*, 2 November 2012. Quickly changed to: 'Is China more legitimate than the West?' It was changed so hurriedly that the new headline didn't make sense: it should have been: 'Is the Chinese government more legitimate than those of the West?'

2. **Could Hitler come to power today?** Unexpectedly asked by the *Economist*, 25 June 2013. It meant in Germany, not here, but the answer was still no.

3. **Is Spongebob Squarepants the new Che Guevara?** Asked by *Vice*, 15 January 2013, about T-shirts seen among Egypt's democracy protesters.

4. **Could Abu Qatada Trigger a Snap General Election?** Simon Heffer in the *Daily Mail*, 27 April 2013.

5. **Are Militant Atheists Using Chemtrails to Poison the Angels in Heaven?** Asked by a poster in a forum on Elite Trader, a website for investors, on 13 July 2013.

6. **Did blowing into Nintendo cartridges really help?** Asked by Chris Higgins, at the Mental Floss website, 24 September 2012. (Actually, he admitted that the answer was no, but it was a great question.)

7. **If everybody in the US drove west, could we temporarily halt continental drift?** Asked by a contributor to the website What If?, 16 April 2013.

8. **Are we literally starving students into submission?** Barbara Ellen, the *Observer*, 25 November 2012. Fewer students turned up for a demo than she thought should have done.

9. **Is this proof the Virgin Queen was an impostor in drag?** *Daily Mail*, 9 June 2013. Joyously at odds with the same newspaper's 2006 headline, 'The proof the Virgin Queen had a secret love child?'

10. **Was the downfall of Richard III caused by a strawberry?** *New Statesman*, 31 August 2013. Something to do with the king acting out of character because of a food allergy.

TRANSPOSITIONS OF SOUNDS IN WORDS

Metathesis is not a thesis about a thesis, but a word that means the shifting of sounds in words, which can happen over time or when a word crosses from one language into another.

1. **Wasp** Used to be waps.

2. **Bird** Used to be brid.

3. **Horse** Used to be hros. Which is impossible to say, so no wonder it changed.

4. **Sashay** An alteration of *chassé*, a ballet movement involving gliding steps with the same foot always leading.

5. **Ask** This has long existed in two forms. Aks was used by Chaucer and is still in use in West Indian vernacular.

6. **Dusk** Used to be dox.

7. **Formaggio** The Italian for cheese inverts *fromage* in French.

8. **Algeria** *Argelia* in Spanish. This is strangely wonderful. David Aaronovitch suggested several other 'so nearly places': Ablania. Buglaria. Svolakia. Atily. Others suggested Kurtey, Vatlia, Aremica and Mendark, which might be near Nomgolia, abutting Nifland.

9. **Third** and **thirteen** The 'r' has moved from its place in 'three'.

10. **Crocodile** *Cocodrilo* in Spanish. My favourite cross-language shift.

I could have had a separate category for people's names. In Nepal Alexander the Great is called Sikander. Cedric was an alteration or misspelling by Walter Scott in *Ivanhoe* of the Anglo-Saxon Cerdic. But the best example comes from the great Francis Wheen:

> I nominate Oprah Winfrey, who was originally called Orpah, after Ruth's sister-in-law in the Old Testament (see book of Ruth, chapter 1).
>
> Here's Oprah's own account:
>
> 'I was born, as I said, in rural Mississippi in 1954. I was born at home. There were not a lot of educated people around and my name had been chosen from the Bible. My Aunt Ida had chosen the name, but nobody really knew how to spell it, so it went down as "Orpah" on my birth certificate but people didn't know how to pronounce it, so they put the "P" before the "R" in every place else other than the birth certificate. On the birth certificate it is Orpah, but then it got translated to Oprah, so here we are.'

WORDS THAT LOST OR GAINED AN 'N'

There are a few words – I could find only ten good examples – that have changed by what the *Oxford Dictionary* calls 'wrong division'.

1. **Apron** Used to be 'napron', from the same French root as napkin. By 'wrong division', 'a napron' was heard as 'an apron'.

2. **Adder** In Old English the snake was called a nædre.

3. **Umpire** Was noumpere in Middle English, from Old French *nonper* 'not equal', that is, a non-participant.

4. **Auger** A tool like a large corkscrew for boring holes in wood. Was nauger, from Old English nafogār, from nafu, wheel-hub, and gār, piercer.

5. **Orange** Seems to have lost its 'n' in Old French, *orenge*, from Arabic *nāranj*.

6. **Nickname** has undergone the opposite change. An eke-name, from eke meaning also, was heard as a neke-name.

7. **Newt** was originally an ewt. But that is quite hard to say, so you can see why it changed.

8. **Nuncle** Archaic or dialect, says the *Oxford Dictionary* – Shakespeare uses it in *King Lear*, 'Can you make no use of nothing, nuncle?' – and dates it from 'late 16th century: by wrong division of mine uncle'.

9. **Nother** This is not just a modern affectation – 'a whole nother thing' – but has been recorded since the 14th century, according to the *OED*.

10. **Notch** 'Probably' from Old French *osche*, according to the *Oxford Dictionary*.

11. The same thing happened to the names Ned and Nell, which come from hearing 'mine Ed', 'mine Ell(en)'.

12. One of the best examples of a similar change borrowing from another language is alligator, which comes from Spanish *el lagarto*, 'the lizard'.

STUPID CAR NAMES

It was the Nissan Qashqai that did it. The dignity of the Triumph Herald and Austin Ambassador of my childhood was being mocked by made-up names. As one correspondent, Joe Crowley, said, 'When I see Qashqai, in my head it always sounds as "cash cow" in a Northern Irish accent.' Here are ten more absurd car names.

1. **Renault Twingo** Nominated by Patrick Hennessy, who also suggested Austin Mini Mayfair and Ford Escort because they were 'named after 1970s porn magazines', but I rejected those.

2. **Mitsubishi Colt Starion** With one 'r'.

3. **Kia cee'd** Not just random textspeak, but an actual name, decided by a marketing department, for a vehicle costing a few thousand pounds.

4. **Mazda Bongo Friendee** Quite magnificent in its multiple strangeness. Almost as weird as its cousin, the Mazda Bongo Brawny.

5. **Nissan Cedric** Popular as taxis in Tokyo, apparently. What makes it stranger is that the name Cedric was invented by Walter Scott as an alteration of Cerdic (see Transpositions of sounds in words, page 72).

6. **Dacia Duster** Sounds great unless you know what it means.

7. **Mitsubishi Carisma** Car. Isma. Clever? No. A bit like the Skoda Superb with added wordplay.

8. **Hyundai Getz** In America, Hyundai rhymes with Sunday.

9. **Ford Ka** Drily witty once. A long time ago in a galaxy far, far away.

10. **VW up!** Volkswagen tries to make everyone write it in lower case with an exclamation mark. It often fails.

Also nominated:

11. Peugeot Bipper Tepee. Not Teepee, because that would be a word.

12. Skoda Yeti

13. Vauxhall Mokka

14. Honda Life Dunk

15. Mohs Ostentatienne Opera Sedan

UNSUNG VILLAINS

Tom Doran started this one with his suggestion for historical figures who don't get as bad a press as they should, and nominated the first on the list. One of my correspondents suggested each one ought to have 'profited from their sociopathology and have at least one Cassandra in their story'. I'm not sure I've kept to that rule, but here is what we came up with:

1. **Erich Ludendorff** Lost the First World War almost single-handed; blamed Jews and Marxists, originating the 'stab in the back' myth; undermined Weimar; and ended up an obscure lunatic too deranged even for Hitler.

2. **Guy Fawkes** 'Terrorist and ally of continental absolutism. Now a cuddly folk hero,' said Matthew Forrest.

3. **Winston Churchill** Nominated by Pete Deveson: 'His successes are well known, but many people don't know about the Bengal famine, or setting troops on miners in the General Strike.'

4. **Che Guevara** 'Mass murderer,' said Dan Fox. 'A megalomaniac who agitated from ideology for a nuclear war that

would have killed millions of his own people,' according to Robert Kaye.

5. **Hugo Chavez** In a similar vein to Guevara. 'Absolutely horrific man and pretend-democrat, who many on the Left still idolise,' said Rob Marchant.

6. **Henry VIII** Nominated by Will Cooling: 'Remembered for his wives but his tyrannical self-obsessed rule leading to more than a century of religious strife is often overlooked.' Joe Skeaping had more to say:

> Henry VIII, who I feel never gets the discredit he deserves for his regime of megalomania and terror, always instead being presented as more of a cartoon villain, a lecherous man who stood up for England.
>
> He should be remembered instead as a genuinely terrifying and unpredictable egomaniac. His break with Rome was an entirely cynical attempt to save his historical reputation from the disasters of his early reign, and it was implemented without regard for the consciences of his subjects or England's diplomatic position. Long-standing royal servants like Wolsey and More were executed for failing to comply with Henry's wishes, he publicly humiliated his wife of over twenty years and his daughter, Mary, introduced new treason laws, presided over show trials and evicted and plundered religious communities that had existed for centuries.

His foreign wars consumed the treasure looted from the Church, leaving England bankrupt and politically isolated. The reign's sole constructive achievement was to give Henry the immortality he craved.

The only doubt about Henry VIII is whether his villainy is unsung enough.

7. **John F. Kennedy** 'An appalling, sleazy, dangerous bastard held up as some kind of hero,' suggested Chris Mochan.

8. **Augustine of Hippo** For the corrosive guilt, self-doubt and shame he embedded, by elaborating the doctrine of original sin so firmly in the Western mind, according to Matthew Tomalin.

9. **Richard I** 'Useless king who spent zero time in England during his reign, and bankrupted the country fighting in the Holy Land,' according to Neil Powell.

10. **Eamon De Valera** 'A terrible human being who is somehow remembered as an Irish hero. And he signed the book of condolence for Hitler's death purely to annoy Britain,' said Kevin Feeney.

LAWS OF LIFE

Whenever I come across an opinion poll that suggests a party has sensationally taken the lead or unexpectedly slumped to a new low, I remember Twyman's Law, named after Tony Twyman, a media-research analyst, which says: 'If a statistic looks interesting or unusual it is probably wrong.' Here are ten other rules for our bewildering world.

1. **Chivers's Law** 'If you can go online and call your government a fascist regime, then you are not living under a fascist regime.'

2. **Godwin's Law** 'As an online discussion grows longer, the probability of a comparison involving Nazis or Hitler approaches 1.'

3. **Conquest's Third Law** 'The simplest way to explain the behaviour of any bureaucratic organisation is to assume that it is controlled by a cabal of its enemies.'

4. **Cowley's Law** 'There is an inverse relationship between the importance of any election campaign technique and the amount of media coverage devoted to it.' Decreed by Professor Philip Cowley.

5. **Rounders' Law** 'If you can't spot the sucker at the poker table in ten minutes, you're the sucker.'

6. **Murphy's Law** 'Anything that can go wrong will go wrong.' Not a piece of casual anti-Irish prejudice, but named after Edward A. Murphy Jr, American aerospace engineer.

7. **Muphry's Law** 'If you write anything criticising editing or proofreading, there will be a fault of some kind in what you have written.'

8. **Pommer's Law** 'A person's mind can be changed by reading information on the internet: from having no opinion to having a wrong opinion.'

9. **Paul's Law** 'You can't fall off the floor.'

10. **Parkinson's Law** 'Work expands so as to fill the time available for its completion.' And its corollary: 'Storage requirements will increase to meet storage capacity.'

Also nominated:

11. Quinlan's Law. 'In matters of military contingency, the expected, precisely because it is expected, is not to be expected.' From Peter Hennessy's book, *Distilling the Frenzy*. The rationale is that what you expect, you plan for, and thus deter. And so all that is left is what you did not deter because you did not expect it.

It was also expounded, in double-bluff form, by Stephen Fry as General Melchett in *Blackadder Goes Forth*:

> MELCHETT: Now, Field Marshal Haig has formulated a brilliant tactical plan to ensure final victory in the field.
> BLACKADDER: Would this brilliant plan involve us

climbing over the top of our trenches and walk-
ing, very slowly, towards the enemy?

DARLING: How did you know that Blackadder? It's
classified information.

BLACKADDER: It's the same plan we used last time,
and the seventeen times before that.

MELCHETT: Exactly! And that is what is so brilliant
about it. It will catch the watchful Hun totally off
guard. Doing exactly what we've done eighteen
times before will be the last thing they expect us
to do this time.

12. Poe's Law. 'Without a winking smiley or other blatant display
of humour, it is impossible to create a parody of fundamentalism that someone won't mistake for the real thing.' According
to Tom Chivers:

It was originally formulated by Nathan Poe in
2005 during a debate on christianforums.com
about evolution, and referred to creationism
rather than all fundamentalism, but has since been
expanded. Poe's Law also has an inverse meaning,
stating that non-fundamentalists will often mistake sincere expressions of fundamentalist beliefs
for parody. Examples abound – one particularly
difficult-to-judge site claims that 'Heliocentrism
[the belief that the Earth orbits the Sun, rather
than the other way around] is an Atheist Doctrine.'

13. Danth's Law (also known as Parker's Law): 'If you have to insist that you've won an internet argument, you've probably lost badly.' Danth was, apparently, a user on the role-playing gamers' forum, RPG.net.

POLITICAL HECKLES

There is an art to heckling, and a good put-down of a heckle is even harder to do well. Given that politics is a branch of stand-up comedy, some of the best practitioners of both heckles and counter-heckles have been elected representatives.

1. **John Wilkes** The 18th-century radical, was once heckled by a man who cried: 'Vote for you? I'd sooner vote for the Devil.' Wilkes replied, 'And what if your friend is not standing?'

2. **Harold Wilson** lauded the nation's maritime glories in a speech. 'And why am I saying all this?' he asked. To which a voice from the back of the hall replied, 'Because you're in Chatham.'

3. **Harold Wilson** said on another occasion: 'The government has no plans to increase public expenditure in Vietnam.' Someone shouted: 'Rubbish!' Wilson: 'I'll come to your special interest in a minute, sir.'

4. A supporter of white rule in Rhodesia once heckled him:

'Why are you talking to savages?' **Harold Wilson**: 'We don't talk to savages. We just let them into our meetings.'

5. I can't find who used it first, and it's not restricted to politics, but it is effective: 'Oh yes, I remember when I had my first drink too.'

6. The next time Margaret Thatcher appeared in the Commons after Geoffrey Howe's deadly resignation speech, **Dennis Skinner**, the Labour MP, called out: 'Hobble, hobble, quack, quack.'

7. **Megan Lloyd George** The Liberal and later Labour MP was heckled by a farmer, who asked if she knew how many ribs a pig had, and replied: 'Come up here and I'll count them.'

8. When Menzies Campbell, 64, on only his second outing as Liberal Democrat leader in 2006, asked a question about pensions, **Eric Forth**, Tory MP, said loudly: 'Declare your interest!'

9. After an MP reminded David Cameron that Claire Rayner had promised to haunt him from beyond the grave if he harmed her beloved NHS, **Labour MPs** kept up a chorus of ghost noises. Maybe you had to be there.

10. 'Is he coming again?' Ironic **Labour tribute** to Cameron's performance at Prime Minister's Questions after he missed three consecutive weekly sessions in 2013 because of other engagements.

An e-petition proposed by David Newham, 'Ban MPs in the House of Commons from heckling and personal attacks and mandate that questions are answered,' was recently rejected because it was 'outside the responsibility of the government'.

BEST BRITISH PLACE NAMES

This list was suggested by Citizen Sane, one of the great assumed identities of the internet, who said that Snodland was where Snods come from.

1. **Splott** In Cardiff.

2. **Pity Me** County Durham.

3. **Bat & Ball** A railway station in Sevenoaks.

4. **Bufflers Holt** Buckinghamshire. Sophie Hannah, the author, said she loved it so much, 'I relocated a character in my new novel so she could live there.'

5. **Warninglid** West Sussex.

6. **Fingringhoe** Essex.

7. **Grimness** Orkney. Once Alex Massie got involved, I realised we could have done a top ten place names, or even a top fifty, in Orkney alone. Orkney also has Riff of Wasbister, Banks of Runabout, Insabysetter, Queefiglamo, Knowes of Euro, Fidge, Candle of the Sneuk, Gump of Spurness, Quackquoy and Hooveth, although I think they just started making

them up at some point in the 1890s. And I could have done another ten just from Shetland: Da Scrodhurdins, Drongi Taing, Fografiddle, Snap, Junk, Hill of Dale, Point of Sluther, Littleness, Rushy Cups and Dud of Flamister.

8. **No Place** Also County Durham.

9. **Ventongimps** A hamlet in Cornwall.

10. **Snodland** Also in Kent.

MOST OVERRATED 1960s BANDS

Chris Deerin, a fellow journalist, is to blame for this one. He complained once that there was 'Doors music being played all over the radio this morning. Just horrible.' When I asked for suggestions of other 1960s bands that were not as good as everyone thinks, John Mullin, my friend and former editor, suggested the Rolling Stones, which of course I ruled out of order.

1. **The Doors** 'Self-regarding yobbery masquerading as mysticism,' according to Andrew Mueller.

2. **The Jimi Hendrix Experience** 'Even Hendrix got cheesed off with the band's deficiencies,' said Mark Pierce.

3. **The Beach Boys** 'Saccharine harmonies, inane lyrics and the same clichés repeated over and over again like a wave hitting the shore.' Robyn Strachan.

4. **Cream** No further comment, your honour.

5. **Fairport Convention** '*Liege and Leaf* got five stars but no one actually played it. Or if they did, they were too stoned to remember.' Karen Buck, Labour MP.

6. **The Monkees** 'The manufactured band that it was all right to like, but not really,' according to Ellen E. Jones.

7. **The Byrds** 'For "Renaissance Fair" alone.' Nuff said, General Boles.

8. **The Velvet Underground** 'The songs featuring Nico make me envy the deaf,' said Citizen Sane.

9. **The Who** 'Otherwise known as The Why,' said Chris Deerin.

10. **The Beatles** Almost by definition, because they are so highly rated.

BEST PRIME MINISTERS WE NEVER HAD

My admiration for Alan Johnson, whose childhood memoir *This Boy* had just been published, prompted a debate about those people who would have made a good prime minister. If A. J. had been a little more arrogant, a little madder, he could have become prime minister in January 2010 and would have continued for another five years, instead of David Cameron. How different, and how much better, that would have been ...

1. **Alan Johnson** Orphan, postman, trade unionist: a one-nation biography and a modernising minister; as with some others on this list, lacked the last ounce of bloodlust.

2. **Michael Heseltine** Would have been more exciting than John Major (and better even than 'the Major we thought we were getting', to quote Ian Leslie), but would have split the Conservatives.

3. **David Blunkett** Could have been the first blind prime minister.

4. **Kenneth Clarke** Unfortunate to come up not just against a Eurosceptic Tory Party, but against Tony Blair.

5. **Hazel Blears** I know, I know, another Blairite (I could have listed John Reid and David Miliband, too). But she is good, and if she hadn't got into trouble with her expenses …

6. **Joseph Chamberlain** Split both the Liberals and the Unionists: imagine if the force of that personality had been deployed in Number Ten.

7. **Barbara Castle** Would have been better than the later Wilson, with the added advantage of pre-empting Thatcher's exceptionalism.

8. **Evan Durbin** Died aged 42 in 1948, rescuing his daughter from the sea. Obscure but with brilliant potential.

9. **Denis Healey** His time came when the Labour Party was off its head and his natural aggression only made matters worse.

10. **Iain Macleod** Never mind the gambling, the money and the women, Macleod was a brilliant centrist who, had he lived, could have replaced Ted Heath in 1972.

VISUAL CLICHÉS

Mark Wallace asked if I could add pictures to my Banned List of clichés, and nominated the first here.

1. Wedding cake decorations for reports and features about gay marriage.

2. Poignant empty swings for stories suggesting that the authorities have failed children.

3. Stretch of police incident tape for any article about crime.

4. The flames from gas-cooker rings for rising energy prices.

5. Faceless greebo lights a gigantic bifta, all but hands and lips obscured, for any story about drugs.

6. The statue on the Old Bailey roof for anything to do with the law or justice.

7. Pictures of people from the neck down for stories about obesity.

8. A woman with her head in her hands for all mental-health stories.

9. Precarious stack of coins for personal finance stories.

10. Aerial montage of suburbia for TV reports on property markets. Used, obviously, because we don't know what houses look like.

USEFUL WORDS FOR WHICH THERE IS NO ENGLISH EQUIVALENT

David Remnick, editor of the *New Yorker*, once described the British as the only nation capable of feeling *Schadenfreude* about themselves. Thus he took a word that isn't even English, but with which we are familiar, and turned it against us. Words in foreign or dead languages are on my Banned List, but some are so useful that they should be admitted on a temporary idiom visa.

1. *Schadenfreude* Joy in the misfortune of others. German.

2. *Wei-wu-wei* Deliberate decision not to do something. Chinese. From an online list compiled by Feedbacq.

3. *Prozvonit* To call a mobile phone to have it ring once so that the other person calls back, saving the first caller money. Czech and Slovak. Allegedly. Someone called Kieran wrote to me: 'I have always used the phrase "drop calling" to describe this exact scenario. I am not the only one; most people here would know what I meant if I said it, maybe it's just a Northern Ireland thing.'

4. *Age-otori* To look worse after a haircut. Japanese.

5. *Chutzpah* Cheek but with self-confident audacity. Yiddish.

6. *Tartle* To hesitate when you cannot remember something, as when you have to introduce someone whose name you cannot recall. Scottish.

7. *Apparatchik* Faceless loyalist in a large political organisation. Russian via German *Apparat*, apparatus.

8. *Esprit de l'escalier* The brilliantly witty response you didn't think of until too late. French.

9. *Fremdschämen* Being embarrassed for someone else, often someone who should be but isn't. Given that English was a half-German pidgin, it is surprising how many words we still have to borrow.

10. *Desenrascanço* To get out of a spot of trouble at the last minute. Portuguese.

POLITICIANS NOT KNOWN BY THEIR FIRST NAME

I could almost have done this list on prime ministers alone: James MacDonald, Arthur Chamberlain, Robert Eden, Maurice Macmillan, James Wilson, Leonard Callaghan and James Brown. But here are ten other politicians:

1. **Boris Johnson** – whose full name is Alexander Boris de Pfeffel Johnson, so you can call him Al.

2. **Vince Cable** – John.

3. **Zac Goldsmith** – Frank.

4. **Keith Vaz** – Nigel.

5. **Paddy Ashdown** – Jeremy John Durham Ashdown acquired the name Paddy when he moved to Bedford School from Northern Ireland when he was eleven.

6. **Enoch Powell** – John, again.

7. **Nick Raynsford** – Wyvill Richard Nicolls Raynsford, minister for London in Tony Blair's government.

8. **Mitt Romney** – who is a Willard, after Willard Marriott, family friend and founder of the hotel chain.

9. **Barbara Follett** – Daphne. The only woman I can find: a minister in Gordon Brown's government and married to Ken, the thriller writer.

10. **Keir Hardie** – Another James.

And some other famous first names: Winifred Mary Beard, Troyal Garth Brooks, Thomas Sean Connery, Joseph Rudyard Kipling, Keith Rupert Murdoch, Helen Beatrix Potter and Adeline Virginia Woolf.

BOOKS PEOPLE BUY
BUT DON'T READ

Ian Rapley quoted an unknown bibliophile to me: 'I don't believe in an afterlife, but I buy books like a man who does.' Few are those indeed who are privileged enough to have reached the end of these:

1. *Long Walk to Freedom* by Nelson Mandela. Millions of copies sold. Millions of spines unbroken.

2. *A Brief History of Time* by Stephen Hawking. Although one correspondent protested that she had read it 'all the way through: it's perfectly easy to do, and the cliché about nobody finishing it is boring'.

3. *Ulysses* by James Joyce. A murky one this, on the grounds that hardly anyone buys it in the first place (you can get it free on Kindle).

4. *Life of Pi* by Yann Martel. 'It's got a tiger in it.' Simon Wilder tried to nominate all Man Booker winners (*Life of Pi* won in 2002), but the excellent Howard Jacobson won in 2010, so I wasn't having that.

5. *Longitude* by Dava Sobel. Nominated by Robert Hutton: 'I keep meaning to.'

6. *Spycatcher* by Peter Wright. A 1980s entry nominated by Verbal Refuse, which may be a code name.

7. *Gravity's Rainbow* by Thomas Pynchon. Nominated by Carl

Engleman, who also tried to nominate Marcel Proust, but people do actually read him.

8. *My Life* by Bill Clinton. So slapdash that long stretches consist of his barely annotated appointments diary.

9. *Living History* by Hillary Rodham Clinton. It would have saved money had the Democratic primary of 2008 been fought as a comparative review of this and Barack Obama's *The Audacity of Hope*.

10. **Any of Jamie Oliver's books.** Nominated by Geraint Whitley, who pointed out that most cookbooks qualify. Except Delia, obviously.

AMERICAN FOOTBALLERS' NAMES

Each year the National Football League holds a three-day ceremony called 'the draft', in which American football teams choose new players from the training grounds of college. Each year the draft is a window on the mostly black American working-class tradition of invented first names, often with French influences, apostrophes and variant spellings.

1. **Barkevious Mingo** Drafted by the Cleveland Browns, his brothers are Hugh and Hughtavious.

2. **Tyrann Mathieu** Drafted by the Arizona Cardinals. Nicknamed 'Honey Badger'. (No, I don't know either.)

3. **D'Brickashaw Ferguson** Drafted in 2006 by the New York Jets. Named after Father Ralph de Bricassart, a character in 1980s TV mini-series *The Thorn Birds*.

4. **Antwaan Randle El** The former Pittsburgh Steeler is retired now, but he was an outstanding player with an equally outstanding name.

5. **Chad Ochocinco** He changed his surname from Johnson to the Spanish for 8-5, the number on his shirt, in 2008.

6. **BenJarvus Green-Ellis** Now with the Cincinnati Bengals, he was nicknamed 'The Law Firm' by his former teammates at the New England Patriots.

7. **LaBrandon Toefield** Formerly with the Jacksonville Jaguars.

8. **Ha'Sean Clinton-Dix** Known as HaHa, he plays for the Green Bay Packers.

9. **Lousaka Polite** Formerly of the Atlanta Falcons and the Miami Dolphins.

10. **Plaxico Burress** The former Pittsburgh Steeler served time after shooting himself in the leg with an unlicensed gun.

Also nominated: Fair Hooker, Richie Incognito, Montavious Stanley, Jerricho Cotchery, Da'Rick Rodgers and Yancey Thigpen.

MISQUOTATIONS

Margaret Thatcher never verifiably said that she regarded New Labour or Tony Blair as her greatest achievement, although it keeps coming up in commentaries about her. Nor can we know that their supposed authors said any of these:

1. **'Because it's there'** – Edmund Hillary. It wasn't him, it was supposedly George Mallory, another climber, although there's no evidence that he said it, either.

2. **'A good day to bury bad news'** – Jo Moore, New Labour special adviser, on 9/11. She wrote: 'It's now a very good day to get out anything we want to bury.'

3. **'When the facts change, I change my mind: what do you do, sir?'** – John Maynard Keynes. No evidence he ever said it. Sorry.

4. **'Elementary, my dear Watson'** – Sherlock Holmes. The character said it in some of the films but Arthur Conan Doyle never wrote it.

5. **'A week is a long time in politics'** – Harold Wilson. No.

6. **'Play it again, Sam'** – as every beginner pedant knows, Ingrid Bergman says 'Play it, Sam' in *Casablanca*.

7. **'Turn if you like. The lady's not for turning'** – Margaret Thatcher. The *New York Times*, writing a notice of her death in 2013, quickly corrected it to 'You turn if you want to…', but the damage to UK ears was done.

8. **'Beam me up, Scotty'** – Captain Kirk never said those precise words when the plot of *Star Trek* required an emergency resuscitation.

9. **'Yo, Blair'** – George W. Bush, when a microphone was left on. Listen to it on the internet and the President clearly says, 'Yeah, Blair'.

10. **'We are intensely relaxed about people getting filthy rich'** – Peter Mandelson. Not a misquotation but a selective one. The rest of the sentence was: '...as long as they pay their taxes.'

WORST BEATLES SONGS

The New Zealand parliament broke into a traditional Maori love song after voting for same-sex marriage. My friend Tom Doran asked what the House of Commons could sing when the Marriage (Same Sex Couples) Bill was passed. Someone suggested, 'All You Need is Love', which Tom rejected on the grounds that it is the Beatles' second-worst song. At which point, I started to compile this list.

1. **'Across the Universe'** Tom Doran: 'The very worst Beatles song is one whose crushing banality and mediocrity are amplified by undeserved acclaim.'

2. **'All You Need is Love'** It's tautological: obviously anything that one can do, can in fact be done.

3. **'Maxwell's Silver Hammer'** As Ian MacDonald wrote in *Revolution in the Head*, 'If any single recording shows why the Beatles broke up…'

4. **'Yellow Submarine'** I don't like it, but Tom put me right. 'It's good for what it is: a novelty kids' song.'

5. **'Octopus's Garden'** Ringo's song. Another one for babies.

6. **'Taxman'** Ben Stanley: 'George Harrison at his misanthropic worst.' Danny Finkelstein replied: 'Are you insane?' And everyone said it is redeemed by Macca's bassline and the intro.

7. **'Christmas Time'** Offered by Rich Greenhill; just avoided being disqualified for obscurity, a rule that excluded 'What's the New Mary Jane' and 'You Know My Name (Look Up the Number)'.

8. **Everything except 'Hey Bulldog'** Fine nomination, although it breaks the previous rule in reverse, in that I had not heard, or heard of, 'Hey Bulldog'.

9. **'Wonderwall'** by Oasis. Yes, very droll, Mark Lott.

10. **'Revolution 9'** Another popular nomination. 'The only one I skip,' said Omer Lev. I was embarrassed to admit that, like anything by Adele, I had never knowingly listened to it.

SURNAMES THAT HAVE DIED OUT

According to ancestry.co.uk and the Guild of One-Name Studies.

1. **Bythewood**

2. **Harred**

3. **Hatman**

4. **Mackmain**

5. **Nithercott**

6. **Pauncefoot**

7. **Raynott**

8. **Rummage**

9. **Temples**

10. **Woodbead**

EVERYDAY LIES

Suggested by David Freedman, who nominated 'Dries your hands in ten seconds' and 'The taxi's at the end of your road now,' and also mentioned Dave Frishberg's song, 'Marooned in a Blizzard of Lies,' from which I have borrowed many of these.

1. 'I was just about to call you.'

2. 'You won't feel a thing.'

3. 'It won't take a minute.'

4. 'I'm coming right away.'

5. 'I'll get right back to you.'

6. 'It's just a standard form.'

7. 'Tomorrow without fail.'

8. 'Pleased to meet you.'

9. 'Your secret's safe with me.'

10. 'He's in a meeting.'

RECURRING NEWS STORIES

Thanks to Is Clutton for this idea. She suggested, 'Last Pit Pony Retires' and 'Previously Unheard Nick Drake Songs Found', which I included to sneak in an extra two before the top ten:

1. 'Leaked details of new *Star Wars* film anger fans.'

2. '"Panther" spotted in Devon.' Followed by, 'Exotic animal not real.'

3. 'American celebrity rumoured to be house-hunting in England.'

4. 'Why can't this country cope with a bit of snow?'

5. 'Cat found safe after 700-mile journey in engine compartment of vehicle.'

6. 'World's oldest person dies.'

7. 'Head teachers call for staggered term times to stop family holiday rip-offs.'

8. 'Fifty-five-year library loan returned: library staff amused and no fine levied.'

9. 'Ed Miliband calls for full independent public inquiry.'

10. 'Putin says soldiers are not Russian.'

There were plenty more good nominations:

11. 'MPs get outrageously long summer holiday.'

12. 'Celebrity wants politics to be different.'

13. 'Postman delivers letter posted in 1971.'

14. 'Cetacean/fish/coelocanth supposed long extinct discovered snacking in waters off Bognor Regis.'

15. 'New Labour dead.'

16. 'Brain drain hits science.' Martyn P. Jackson, who commented: 'Somehow we always seem to survive every catastrophic brain drain and continue to produce Nobel prize winners.'

17. 'New dinosaur discovered (looks like a chicken).'

18. 'Cure for obesity found.'

19. 'Have-a-go granny fights off robber with handbag.'

20. 'Met Office disastrously wrong.'

21. 'Killer wasps from continent.'

22. 'Opposition's sums don't add up.'

23. 'Government department has travel expenses.'

24. 'Japanese soldier discovered on island still fighting WW2.'

25. 'Is this a photo of the Loch Ness Monster?'

26. 'Rolling Stones To Tour For Last Time.'

27. 'World's oldest man/woman smokes fifty a day/drinks daily bottle of whisky/lives on dripping sandwiches and pork pies.'

Then there are a number of binary alternative stories:

28. 'A-level/GCSE record results/dumbed down outrage.'

29. 'Pregnancy brain does/does not exist.'

30. 'Drinking in pregnancy is good/bad for the baby.'

31. 'Home birth is safe/deadly.'

32. 'British songbirds nearly extinct/returning in droves.'

YIDDISH WORDS

Matt Hoffman noodged me to do this one. Chutzpah features elsewhere in 'Useful words for which there is no English equivalent' (page 90), which is just as well, because competition for these ten places was fierce.

1. **Shpilkes** Agitated, as in waiting for exam results.

2. **Shtum** Silent, with a few layers of extra meaning, as with most of these.

3. **Kvetch** Complain, complainer.

4. **Schlemiel** Awkward, unlucky person.

5. **Verklempt** or **farklempt** Overwrought.

6. **Schlep** Long and tedious journey, noun or verb.

7. **Nosh** Originally a snack bar.

8. **Schmooze** Originally a long and intimate chat.

9. **Zimzoom** Mosquito.

10. **Noodge** To pester. In Britain and US influenced by nudge. Verb and noun, although Polish Yiddish also has *noodnik* or *nudnik*, a pest.

I also quite like these:

11. Hoika fensta. Literally 'high window'. Someone rich who lived on the upper floors of the ghetto.

12. Kolboynik. A rascally know-it-all.

13. Kosher. In the sense of 'proper', 'pukka'.

14. Mensch. A person of integrity and honour.

15. Nebbish, nebech. One who is fearful and timid, especially in making decisions and plans, in discussions, debates, arguments, and confrontations, and in taking responsibility. Often has to clean up after a schlemiel.

16. Schmaltz. Excessive sentimentality. Oxford Dictionary dates it to the 1930s: from Yiddish *shmaltz*, German *Schmalz* 'dripping, lard'.

17. Shvuntz. Useless person, coward.

ELEGANT VARIATIONS

Lloyd Bracey started this game of inverting or altering clichés to make them fresh again (a cliché originally being a stencil).

1. **Yes-brainer**

2. **A might-read**

3. **A shoo-out**

4. **Rare sense**

5. **A foregone introduction**

6. 'If at first you don't succeed, try two more times so that your failure is statistically significant.'

7. **A flawed storm**

8. **That's a taken**

9. **In empty flow**

10. **Auto-incorrect**

Other ingenious offerings included:

11. A tame goose chase. The original version is one of many phrases first found in Shakespeare.

12. With the benefit of foresight

13. Someone who doesn't suffer experts gladly

14. Wake up and smell the rose hip tea

15. If you miss only one film this year, make it this one

16. Let's inaction that

17. This proposal is a panacea

GREAT UNREMARKED CHANGES OF OUR LIFETIME

This list was suggested by Andrew Denny, who was responsible for the first item. Sorry if it is basically a lot of old people saying, 'You don't know how lucky you are.'

1. **Duvets replaced sheets and blankets in the 1970s**

2. **Nobody phones mum and dad with three rings any more**

3. **Rolling luggage**

4. **Street design** Getting rid of pedestrian railings, mostly.

5. **Wine used to be only occasional, sweet and in tiny glasses. Coffee used to be only instant and horrible.**

6. **People clean up after their dogs (usually)**

7. **The end of lunchtime drinking**

8. **The Flynn Effect: we've been getting more intelligent for 80 years.** This is true. Or, at least, average IQ scores have been rising – at about three points a decade on average.

9. **It used to be only the urban rich who could buy out of season. Now it's only the urban rich who want to buy in season.**

10. **The annual number of deaths on UK roads has fallen by two thirds in thirty years**

Some nominations were obscure. Many people will have no idea, for example, what 'poste restante' was: a way of sending letters to a post office in some faraway part of the world to be collected by a traveller. Cars don't backfire anymore; cheques will soon be phased out (they are still used a lot in America, according to Arieh Kovler); there used to be things called filofaxes; and chocolate, wrapped in aluminium foil, used to be sold in vending machines that worked about fifty per cent of the time in stations.

My colleague Matt Chorley nominated sauces sold in squeeze bottles and stamps and envelopes which require no licking.

Finally I nominated the London Tube, now the best mass transit system in the world, but this might be a little London-centric and in any case met some customer resistance from other passengers. However, my friend Janan Ganesh backed me up: 'London's overall transport infrastructure – bus, Tube, the new Overground, Eurostar, City airport, Heathrow Express – is now world class.'

TOP TEN LISTS THAT DIDN'T MAKE IT

And finally, here are some of my best false starts. So many good ideas, but not all of them made it through the entire production process to emerge as a complete 'ten'. Mathematical proof of Rentoul's Theorem: If at first you don't succeed, try something else.

Ways to outwit Sherlock Holmes I thought it would be easy to come up with ten of these, given how slapdash Arthur Conan Doyle was about the original and those ridiculous mixed-up Tube trains in Steven Moffat's tribute television series. Besides, Conan Doyle's Holmes seemed to supply a fitting aphorism for this book: 'It has long been an axiom of mine that the little things are infinitely the most important.'

Some of the work had even been done for me, by Ronald Knox, in an article called 'Studies in the Literature of Sherlock Holmes', originally published in *The Blue Book*, 1910, which is, rather wonderfully, available on the internet. It was Knox who pointed out that in 'The Man With the Twisted Lip', Mrs Watson addresses her husband as James, when everyone knows his name is John. Knox records drily that some Sherlockians have suggested this is a clue to the existence of a second Watson, which may explain some of the other inconsistencies in Conan Doyle's work.

It may be, for example, that the Watson who says, in *A Study in Scarlet*, that Holmes's knowledge of literature and philosophy was 'nil' is a different person from the Watson who later records

Holmes comparing Hafiz with Horace, quoting Tacitus, Flaubert, Goethe, and Thoreau, and reading Petrarch in a railway carriage.

The first Watson has a war wound in his shoulder, whereas the later one is troubled by the same thing in his leg.

Unfortunately, however, Knox loses interest in mere blooper-spotting and his essay diverts into a fine affectionate analysis of the eleven parts of the ideal type of Sherlock Holmes story:

> The first part is the Prooimion, a homely Baker Street scene, with invaluable personal touches, and sometimes a demonstration by the detective. Then follows the first explanation, or Exegesis, that is, the client's statement of the case, followed by the Ichneusis, or personal investigation, often including the famous floor-walk on hands and knees.

And so on.

Conan Doyle enjoyed Knox's teasing, admitting that 'you know a great deal more about it than I do, for the stories have been written in a disconnected (and careless) way without referring back to what had gone before'. He regarded his Holmes stories as ephemeral entertainment: he wanted to be remembered for his historical romances. Don't we all.

But he also pre-empted nit-pickers and plot-holers by having Holmes admit to mistakes and suggest that Watson, who is the narrator and supposed chronicler of his friend's exploits in most of the stories, had flattered him. In 'Silver Blaze', the story with the curious incident of the dog in the nighttime, a prize horse goes missing. Some pedants point out that the silence of the dog did not necessarily mean that it knew the intruder: could the thief not have come armed with sausages? But Conan Doyle got there before them. As Holmes and Watson head to Dartmoor to help with the investigation, Holmes mentions that on Tuesday evening, the horse's owner and the police had telegraphed for his assistance on the case. Watson says, 'Tuesday evening! And this is Thursday morning. Why didn't you go down yesterday?'

To which Holmes replies, 'Because I made a blunder, my dear Watson – which is, I am afraid, a more common occurrence than anyone would think who only knew me through your memoirs. The fact is that I could not believe it possible that the most remarkable horse in England could long remain concealed, especially in so sparsely inhabited a place as the north of Dartmoor.'

As for the television series, Holmes and Watson investigate CCTV footage showing a man boarding a Jubilee line train to travel one stop between Westminster and St James's Park, which are connected by the District and Circle Lines. Later, Benedict Cumberbatch and Martin Freeman walk along a section of the Piccadilly Line to a stationary train that has been rigged with explosives which is supposedly underneath the Houses of Parliament.

However, Steven Moffat, the creator of *Sherlock*, disarmed the critics when people tried to find fault with Holmes faking his death:

> I don't know what they're talking about, I thought it was watertight. What were they complaining about? I think people have come to think a plot hole is something which isn't explained on screen. A plot hole is actually something that can't be

explained. Sometimes you expect the audience to put two and two together for themselves. For *Sherlock*, and indeed *Doctor Who*, I've always made the assumption that the audience is clever.

So at that point I had to accept that it is not possible to outwit Sherlock.

Overused statistics constructs A fine idea of Rob Macpherson's, who had had enough of things being 'the size of Wales', especially as, as Bob From Brockley pointed out, most people outside Wales, and many inside it, have no idea how big Wales is. Even more especially, as Jeff Gazzard pointed out, once it has been translated into the metric system of areas the size of Belgium. How many football pitches is that? As I mulled this over, the newspapers reported the discovery of the fossil bones of a new largest dinosaur, the height of a several-storey building and the length of lots of London buses (although buses in London are pretty much the same size as those in most other places now that Boris Johnson has got rid of the bendy ones). Then a news release arrived from the Cabinet Office about property disposals: 'Government gets out of property twenty-six times the size of Buckingham Palace.' As James Chapman commented, 'You could fill three Albert Halls, lay them end to end and reach to the Moon and back.' Finally, Qiffypedia pointed out: 'Every year, an area the size of Wales is next to England.' So I thought it best to move on.

Misattributed quotations I did top ten Misquotations, but Rich Greenhill found that 'Give me lucky generals', usually attributed to Napoleon Bonaparte, originated with Cardinal Mazarin, chief minister of France 1642–1661. He is quoted by Denis Diderot in *Encyclopédie Ou Dictionnaire Raisonné Des Sciences, Des Arts Et Des Métiers*, 1756, as saying that the question to ask of a general is not, '*Est-il habile?*' Is he skilful? but, '*Est-il heureux?*' Is he lucky? Now I just need nine more.

Sonorous inversions This is what I call phrases such as 'have your cake and eat it'. The meaning is really 'eat your cake and [still] have it', but it sounds wrong, so we say it the other way round and every now and again someone says, 'But that doesn't make sense.' Another common one is 'head over heels': it is the wrong way round, but the vowels and consonants don't work in 'heels over head'. Then there is 'thunder and lightning': everyone knows that you see the lightning first because light travels faster than sound, but try saying 'lightning and thunder'. I couldn't find another seven.

Disgusting student foods The most shocking fact in a recent edition of the *Independent on Sunday* was that three per cent of people admit to using peanut butter as a pasta sauce. No, that is not 'satay', it is the sort of horrible food that young people eat once. I used to have butter and marmalade on Weetabix biscuits. Lynsey Hopkins admitted that, 'as a student, I made a beef and tomato pot noodle with water from the hot tap. Mixed results.' Citizen Sane confessed that, when he was a student, hungry at around midnight, he was reduced to sugar on buttered toast, and claimed that his housemate used to make toast by holding bread up against the grill of the gas fire in his room. Jane Merrick used to eat fish finger sandwiches. With ketchup. Stephen Pollard said a 'former flatmate' (as in 'asking for a friend', I expect) used to have Fruit 'n Fibre smeared with taramasalata. Too revolting to go any further.

Sports that weren't invented by the British This was a fine idea, suggested by Andrew Denny, who nominated *buzkashi*, a central Asian sport in which horse-mounted players drag a goat carcass towards a goal. Stuart Neale offered *jai alai*, 'a kind of pelota' played in the Basque country (which baffled me, because pelota itself is a Basque game). Paul Cotterill and Gillian Joseph both nominated *kabaddi*, an ancient Indian wrestling game, the national game of Bangladesh and the state game of Tamil Nadu in India. And Mary Novakovich nominated handball. This was first played in Denmark in the late 19th century. The rules were codified in Scandinavia and Germany. But that was it. There are just not that many sports worth playing that were invented outside the British Isles.

Joy-giving lines in English literature I thought this was a brilliant idea of Chris Deerin's. He asked: 'Is there a more joy-giving line in English literature than "Feather-footed through the plashy fen passes the questing vole"?' Then I looked it up. I had forgotten that it was Evelyn Waugh's instance of the overwritten style of a certain kind of journalist – in this case William Boot in *Scoop*. So I wasn't sure if Chris was praising the genius of Waugh's pastiche or if he just liked it anyway. Then Ruth Davidson, the leader of the Conservatives in the Scottish Parliament, nominated the non-ironic line, 'your kiss, recalled, unstrings, like pearls, this chain of words', by Carol Ann Duffy, 'Rapture', 2005. 'Perfect for that stomach-flipping feeling leaving you lost,' said Davidson. These being deep waters, I decided, feather-footed, to tiptoe away.

Best SI units Tom Doran proposed this list and nominated his three favourites: the henry (unit of inductance), the coulomb (electric charge) and the lumen (luminous flux). The trouble is that there are only seven base units in the *Système International* and twenty-two derived units, most of them taken from people's surnames. A top ten would therefore merely be the best third. Scrap that idea.

Countries with no name Since Czechoslovakia split, the Czech Republic has been an anomalous country, in that Czech is a well-known adjective, and a Czech is a person from there, but there is no one word for the country. The Basque country is the only other example that occurs to me.

Maths jokes There are 10 types of people in the world: those who understand binary numbers and those who don't. That is one of my favourites. As is this one: fx walks into a bar – 'I'm sorry, sir,' said the bartender, 'we don't cater for functions.' But if I wanted to write a joke book, I would have to think of some new jokes rather than reprinting old ones, so I abandoned that idea.

TOP TEN PEOPLE TO WHOM I AM GRATEFUL (OTHERWISE KNOWN AS 'THE ACKNOWLEDGEMENTS')

1. Laurence Earle, who was editor of the *New Review*, the *Independent on Sunday*'s magazine. He liked some of the lists and curios on my blog and asked if I could do something like them for the back page. He may have used the word 'interactive' but I think that was all right because it really is.

2. Mike Higgins, Laurence's successor, who didn't scrap it.

3. Lisa Markwell, editor of the *Independent on Sunday*, who indulges my foibles and even lets me ban things such as hashtags, selfies and hipsters in the news pages of the newspaper.

4. All my other wonderful colleagues at the *Independent* and the *Independent on Sunday*.

5. My colleagues in the parliamentary press gallery: a remarkable group of people. Donald Macintyre once told me of a PhD about competitive co-operation among political journalists. One of these days I will try to find it.

6. Olivia Bays, Jennie Condell and Pippa Crane at Elliott & Thompson.

7. Robert Bruce, Hugh Stephenson, John Lloyd, David Aaronovitch, Glenwyn Benson, David Jordan, Ian Hargreaves, Andrew Marr, Rosie Boycott, Simon Kelner, Tristan Davies

and John Mullin, my editors over the years from whom I have learned so much.

8. You will have noticed that this is already more than ten people.

9. All the readers of the *Independent on Sunday*, my Twitter account and the *Independent* blog (see page 117 for a list of those who contributed to this book). As with *The Banned List* and *Questions To Which The Answer Is No*, I am merely the curator of your collective genius.

10. You, the reader, or whoever paid for this copy of the book.

CONTRIBUTIONS AND NOMINATIONS

Page 1 Underrated family films: 2. Mark Wallace; 3 and 4. Professor Paul Cairney; 5. Tom Doran; 6. Gaz W.; 10. Isabel. **Page 2 Plurals that have become singular:** 19. Alan Robertson. **Page 6 Malapropisms:** 5. Alistair Gray; 9. Lloyd Bracey; 10 Hugh Kellett; 13. Jane Merrick; 15. Roger Stevenson; 16. Peter Metcalfe; 17. Lisa Markwell. **Page 8 Signs with double meanings:** 2. Andrew Denny; 6. Tony Hall; 7. David Artley; 8. From Citizen Sane; 9. Mike Graham; 10 Nick Thornsby; 13. Jenifer Jeffery; 17. Fred Walker; 18. Peter Shearman; 20. Simon Cox. **Page 10 Surprisingly unrelated pairs of words:** 4. Edmund W. **Page 12 First sentences of novels:** 5. Sarah Wollaston MP. **Page 19 Words that used to mean the opposite:** 10. Della Mirandola; 11. Francis Wheen. **Page 22 Fictional villains:** 5. Andy McSmith; 6. Mark Lott. **Page 23 Upbeat songs that tell a sad story:** Clive Davis; 2. Omer Lev; 3. Truly S; 4. Emma Burnell; 5. Jill Rutter; 6. Ben Stanley; 7. Jonathan Portes; 8. Sara Morris/Luke Hurst; 9. Truly S. **Page 25 Genuine shop names:** 7. Gary Plumb; 31. James Whetlor; 32. Ryan Bourne; 34. Tom Doran; 36. Darren Murphy; 38. and 39. Big Gaz; 41. Jo Barrow; 50. Jamie Thunder. **Page 28 Mixed metaphors:** 3. Frank (Twitter). **Page 30 Lost positives:** 1. Mark Wallace; 8. Michael Crick; 9. Karl Turner; 10. Sam Freedman. **Page 37 Tautologies:** 21. Ramesh Biswas. **Page 41 Songs that mean the opposite of what most people think:** 5. Jem Stone; 6. Giles Coren; 11. Stella Creasy MP; 13. James Chapman; 15. Rob Davies; 18. William French; 20. Clive Davis. **Page 45 Most English remarks of all time:** 4. Sean Kenny; 9. Mark Wallace. **Page 47 Misused fables:** 6. Colin Rosenthal. **Page 48 Palindromes:** 2. Chris Deerin; 3. Palindromelist.net; 6. Isabel; 11. Stig Abell. **Page 49 Words used only with one other word:** 1, 8, 11 and 14. Tom Freeman; 2. Arieh Kovler; 3 and 20. Stewart Wood; 4. Steve Van Riel; 5. David Crosbie; 6. Danny Kemp; 7. Andy McSmith; 9. Peter Campbell; 10 and 12. Joel Carter; 16. Ten-Acre Wines; 18. Michael Crick; 20. Stewart Wood. **Page 51 English Monarchs 1066–1707:** 3. Michael McCarthy; 4. David Head; 5. Louise McCudden; 8. John Blake; 9. Alex Massie; 10. Ian Silvera.

Page 55 Most beautiful British railway journeys: 2. Bob Reid; 4. Paul T. Horgan; 8. Andrew Adonis. **Page 57 Phrases that ought to be off the menu:** 4. Sadie Smith; 5. John West. **Page 58 Words that ought to be used more often:** 9. Jessica Elgot. **Page 62 Great bands with terrible names:** 1. Tom Doran; 6. Stuart Ritchie; 10. Peter A. Russell. **Page 63 Films panned as turkeys that are actually quite good:** 1, 3, 6 and 9. Richard T. Kelly; 2. Pete Hoskin; 4. Gabriel Milland; 5. Alex Massie; 7. Lee Ravitz; 8. Joe H.; 10. Larry Ryan. **Page 65 Political myths:** 2. Tom Doran. **Page 67 Original titles of novels:** 2. Richard T. Kelly; 11. Daniel Hannan and Mark Wallace. **Page 74 Words that lost or gained an 'N':** 11. James Chapman. **Page 75 Stupid car names:** 1. Patrick Hennessy. **Page 77 Unsung villains:** 2. Matthew Forrest; 3. Pete Deveson; 4. Dan Fox; 5. Rob Marchant; 6. Will Cooling; 7. Chris Mochan; 8. Matthew Tomalin; 9. Neil Powell; 10. Kevin Feeney. **Page 85 Best British place names:** 7. Alex Massie. **Page 86 Most over-rated 1960s bands:** 1. Andrew Mueller; 2. Mark Pierce; 3. Robyn Strachan; 5. Karen Buck; 6. Ellen E. Jones; 7. General Boles; 8. Citizen Sane; 9. Chris Deerin. **Page 89 Visual clichés:** 1. Mark Wallace. **Page 90 Useful words for which there is no English equivalent:** 2. Feedbacq. **Page 91 Politicians not known by their first name:** 9. Ken Penton. **Page 93 Books people buy but don't read:** 4. Simon Wilder; 5. Robert Hutton; 6. Verbal Refuse; 7. Carl Engleman; 10. Geraint Whitley. **Page 94 American footballers' names:** 1. Mark Henderson. **Page 96 Misquotations:** 3. Rob Hutton. **Page 97 Worst Beatles songs:** 1, 4. Tom Doran; 6. Ben Stanley; 8. Hegemony Jones; 9. Mark Lott; 10. Omer Lev. **Page 99 Everyday lies:** 1. Neil Walker; 2. Allan Draycott. **Page 100 Recurring news stories:** 11. Rick Toomer; 12. Tom Freeman; 13. David Freeman; 14. Armand D'Angour; 15. John Blake; 16. Martyn P Jackson; 20. Mark Wallace; 21. James Landale; 22 and 23. Steve Van Riel; 24. Spinning Hugo; 25. Brian Spanner; 26. Rob Marchant; 27. The Dabbler; 28: Tim Bale/Dan Kelly. **Page 104 Elegant variations:** 3. Neal Baker; 4, 5 and 9. Andy Cowper; 6. Sam Freedman; 8. Brian Spanner; 10. Paul Staines (aka Guido Fawkes); 12. Andy Cowper; 13. Louise Ankers; 14. David Freedman; 15. Alan Beattie; 16. Carl Baker; 17. Michael McGough. **Page 106 Great unremarked changes of our lifetime:** 1. Andrew Denny; 8. Dan Fox; 10. Mark Bassett